A Century of Powerful Disney Insights

Volume I
1923-1973
The Walt & Roy Disney Years

Written by

J. Jeff Kober

Performance Journeys Publishing

Performance Journeys publishes its books in a variety of print and electronic formats. Some content that appears in one format may not appear in another.

Editor: Terry Czigan
Graphics: Justin Rucker

ISBN 979-8-218-28338-4

Printed in the United States of America
Performance Journeys Publishing | www.PerformanceJourneys.com
Address queries to jeffkober@gmail.com

To my wife Kathy,

Whose love and care cannot be quantified. No one in this world completes my life more than her.

Ours is not 100 years—it's an eternity.

Table of Contents

Preface

October 16, 1923

Disney and I share something fundamentally in common—the same birthdate. Most know "D23" as a combination of both Disney and 1923, the year the organization was founded. Trust me, I don't share that year in common! But most don't know that the day the organization was founded was October 16th, which is also the same month and day I was born. I came to learn that fact in 1973, on the 50th anniversary of the company. The year prior I had found a used 1963 National Geographic magazine in the library which had an article on Disney. The pages unfolded in a way that riveted my young self to the magical worlds of Walt Disney. We were already going to California for summer vacation. I asked my parents if we could go up to Disneyland during the week. They obliged and the rest was history. I had earlier experiences at Disneyland, but my senses came alive as I found courage to visit the Haunted Mansion for the first time, see the new Bear Country and experience the Main Street Electrical Parade. It was a touchstone experience I can't begin to describe. At the age of twelve I started writing the company letters—I wanted to work there—I wanted to be part of the magic when I grew up. They corresponded with me, sending park guides, press releases and maps. One item sent was a placard celebrating 50 Happy Years of Family Entertainment. When I realized the company was founded on the same day I was born, I knew that the cosmos had put us together.

Over the last several years, as the 100th Anniversary of the Walt Disney Company approached, I considered writing a book that celebrated the vision, ideas, and takeaways of this great organization. I had already written several books, and had ideas for several more, but this one kept coming to the forefront. I knew that however the anniversary would be celebrated, I wanted to do something on this anniversary that would give meaning well beyond it.

So, with all of that in mind, I started to write this book. I wrote. And I wrote. In doing so I was particularly keen that key individuals, films, and events would not be missed. There are many books that cover Walt Disney. There are books focused on Disneyland and Walt Disney World. There are books that center on Michael Eisner and Bob Iger. There are even books examining specific events like the 1941 strike or the New York World's Fair. But few books canvas the entire 100 years. This is one of those few works. Yes, there are many new insights to even the biggest Disney fan. But while encompassing, it is prose with a purpose. I want each story to inspire. I want each milestone to share insight and impart understanding to our lives. I want to offer ideas for the next century.

100 Years of Struggle & Joy

There are reasons why this organization shouldn't be here today. It has experienced conflict, difficulty, and challenges. I present the reality of that. It's part of the tale, and I don't shy away from the truth that some things should not have happened. But at the heart of this story, is that a great vision, along with the strength and determination of an entire team working together, can truly create an amazing accomplishment. This is not about some perfect company—but an imperfect band of dreamers and doers led by the leadership of a man who knew a little something about making dreams come true.

Nearly 300 pages in I knew I had a problem. There is so much to cover! The world of Disney is fascinating, insightful, and full of important milestones. I kept trying to figure out how I could edit back—make it leaner. And then it struck me. This was two books. One clearly was centered around the Roy and Walt Years. The second would be how the years of Card Walker and Ron Miller would lead to Michael Eisner and then all the way through to Bob Iger—both times! And the 100th wasn't even over! So, this is Volume I. I hope you love it! Moreover, I hope it inspires you whether you are a fan, or whether you are just being introduced to the Disney legacy. There are so many fascinating tales to share. Walt Disney was about storytelling, and this is a story worth telling!

7

To that end, I celebrate 100 years of Disney Magic, and dedicate this volume to the two who started it all on October 16, 1923:

To Walt and Roy Disney, who have sought to bring "happily ever after" to the lives of so many. This book is dedicated to the profound way you have influenced the world around us. Thank you for what you created in the first 50 years that have given us the entire 100 years. And most of all, thank you for the ideas and inspiration that will lead us into the next 100 years.

1

Walt Arrives in California

What Can You Do with Just a Suitcase and a Dream?

"A suitcase and a dream" are how people often refer to the "Storytellers" statue at the end of Buena Vista Street in Disney California Adventure. Captured just life size is a bronze image of Mickey and Walt heading into California to pursue a new life. As Walt stated:

> It was July 1923. I packed all of my worldly goods—a pair of trousers, a checkered coat, a lot of drawing materials and the last of the fairy tale reels we had made—in a kind of frayed cardboard suitcase. And with that wonderful audacity of youth, I went to Hollywood, arriving there with just forty dollars. It was a big day the day I got on that Santa Fe California Limited. I was just free and happy!

Of course, Mickey's not there yet. That won't happen until 1928. This is 1923, and it's just months before October 16th, when Walt will move forward with a new business. At this point when Walt left Missouri for California, he had something better than a mouse waiting for him. He had his brother Roy. Together, what brought them to this moment prior to October 16th was a lot more ominous than just a suitcase and a dream.

It was more like bankruptcy, illness, and unemployment.

Bankruptcy

Bankruptcy was not in very young Walt's plans. Rather, he had established a company known as Laugh-O-Grams that produced one-minute cartoons—a sort of program filler for small, neighborhood theaters. He started doing shorts based on fairy tales like Little Red Riding Hood and Jack and the Beanstalk. But beyond the deposit, the distributor never made a payment, and Walt quickly became broke. A local dentist, Thomas B. McCrum, inquired about having a film produced to promote dental health. For $500 Walt created *Tommy Tucker's Tooth*.

But Walt was looking for something more. A cartoon competitor, Max Fleischer, had created an *Out of the Inkwell* series that portrayed animated cartoons in a physical world. Walt thought to reverse that by putting a human figure in a cartoon world. He would call it *Alice's Wonderland*, but he ran out of money trying to finish it. To that end, he wrote Margaret Winkler, a leader in the silent animation business of the 1920's, who agreed to purchase and distribute the film, that he simply didn't have the money. He would soon go into bankruptcy proceedings that would nag him until creditors received 45 percent of their claim years later. Meanwhile he needed a new start, but where?

Illness

The specter of illness wasn't about Walt. It was about his brother Roy who was already in California. And it was an infectious disease that sent him there. He had been back in Kansas City working at First National Bank, close to Walt as they had been growing up. Roy was dating Edna, and they were looking toward the prospects of marriage. That was about the time that he came down with influenza—twice. The doctor thought Roy needed his tonsils removed. Roy and Walt's brother Herb recommended a doctor who could remove them over lunch, so Roy wouldn't have to miss work. But after the procedure he began to hemorrhage, and Herb took Roy to the hospital.

The doctor may have been a quack, but the hospital X-rays revealed a spot located on Roy's lung. It was tuberculosis, probably acquired while Roy was serving in the Navy. He was assigned to a veteran's hospital in Santa Fe, New Mexico, then transferred to another one in Tucson, Arizona. Roy found Santa Fe too cold and Tucson too hot. When he felt well enough, he came to Glendale, California, outside of Los Angeles and adjacent to Burbank. There he suffered another relapse and was assigned to a hospital in west Los Angeles. Still, he corresponded with Walt who was desperate in Kansas City, "Kid, I think you should get out of there. I don't think you can do any more for it."

Unemployment

In July of 1923, Walt came with a suitcase and a dream, and was very much unemployed. He moved in with his Uncle Robert, then went to visit his brother Roy, who was concerned about his brother's skinniness. "Hey kid, haven't you been eating? I'm supposed to be the sick one. So now that you're in L.A. what are you going to do with yourself?"

Walt replied: "I don't know. I've given up on animation. But I've got to get into show business somehow. I think I'll try and become a director."

Walt, who had filmed some newsreel footage in Kansas City, printed a business card stating he was a member of the press, and used it to get past the studio gates. At one point he had a meeting with a secretary at Metro. "Yes. I had my own studio in Kansas City. I made cartoons and live-action films. Perhaps you heard of me?"

The secretary's response? "No. I can't say that I have."

In Bob Thomas's biography, he notes Roy as saying about Walt:

> Tomorrow was always going to be the answer to all his problems…During the period before he got his [cartoon] contract, he was hangin' around this town and I kept saying

to him, 'Why don't you get a job?' And he could have got a job, I'm sure, but he didn't want a job.

He'd get into Universal, for example, on the strength of applying for a job. Then when he'd get out of the office, he'd just hang around the studio all day and go over on some sets and see what was going on. MGM was another favorite spot where he could work that gag...But he had a persistency, and optimism about him all the time. A drive.

While Walt thought the best chance of having a cartoon business was back in New York, Roy persisted with the idea of Walt going back to making pictures. Taking the *Alice's Wonderland* picture he had done in Kansas City, Walt considered a new series based on Alice. Margaret Winkler made him an offer. Roy had saved money from his disability pension and put in $200. The brothers went to their uncle for an advance of $500 to get them started. Their parents, Elias and Flora, also put a mortgage on their home in Portland and loaned them $2,500. It was primarily their family who helped them out.

Bankruptcy, illness, and unemployment. These are the circumstances that led up to their watershed moment of October 16th, 1923. Walt and Roy signed a contract with M. J. Winkler for the distribution of six initial *Alice Comedies* for a price of $1,500 a piece, and six more at $1,800 apiece, with an option for two more series.

The Suitcase & The Dream

And what about "a suitcase & a dream"?

The dream represented everything that a future and a new beginning could bring. A new start. New opportunities. New hope. The suitcase was cardboard and held extraordinarily little contents inside it. But what it really held was what Walt had learned at that time: Perseverance. Family. Optimism.

The statue at Disney California Adventure is positioned in a quite different way than the elevated Partners statues that sit in front of castles at Disneyland, Walt Disney World, and elsewhere. It's still

Mickey and Walt, but it's a seasoned pair that represents success and what can be accomplished when working together hand in hand. The *Suitcase & a Dream* "Storytellers" statue sits at ground level and subtly suggests that Walt is no different than you and me. We can build our own future with our dreams and the life experiences we hold in our hands and heart.

Perseverance. Family. Optimism. If Walt could do it. You can do it.

Ideas for the Next Century

Consider how you can make the magic come alive for you:

- What circumstances surrounding you *now* are moving you toward change?

- What life experiences are packed inside *your* suitcase?

- What is the dream that gives *you* hope, determination, and persistence?

- Instead of seeing *tomorrow* as the answer to your problems, can you seek and find it in *today*?

2

Humble California Beginnings

What Basics Are Needed for Success?

Starting from Scratch

Most outsiders assume that the success of any legendary organization stems from the fact that they had plenty of resources to accomplish extraordinary results. The thinking goes: they spent their way to success.

The truth can often be just the opposite. The humble beginnings of some of the most renowned companies may surprise you, and how the hard lessons of being resourceful were (and are) a source of competitive advantage.

Besides working with computers, what do Steve Jobs and Steve Wozniak of Apple, Bill Hewlett, and David Packard all have in common? The answer is that all four started their phenomenal companies in a garage. And they're not the only ones—Elliot and Ruth Handler of Mattel did, C.E. Woolman started what became Delta Airlines out of a gas-station garage, and DeWitt and Lila Wallace nurtured Reader's Digest from a garage apartment.

And Walt Disney: he began in his uncle's garage. Even before getting official word from Margaret Winkler to re-start the *Alice* series, he found an animation camera and set it up in his uncle's garage while trying to figure it out by tinkering with the camera. As events unfolded, the brothers set up shop in the back of a small office

14

on Kingswell Avenue. When a little more money came in, they moved to their own little office, also on Kingswell Avenue. Three years later they would build what would become a larger, sprawling studio on Hyperion. Walt and Roy were in business for more than 15 years before they would build their "ideal" office setting in 1940. But before that moment came, some of their most remarkable work would take place in the most makeshift of settings, beginning with that garage.

Great Things Happen in Garages

Make no mistake, there is nothing inherently special about the physical "aesthetic" of a garage; it simply acts as a bare bones' incubator for possibilities. Starting with only the essentials, the musician, the artist, the inventor, the cartoonist becomes focused on building upward and onward. Sparse surroundings can help focus the attention to reject the status quo in search of the next big breakthrough. The austerity fosters the spirit of entrepreneurship that sometimes can't be addressed in the distracting trappings of a fine office building.

You see this same thing played out at the top of *Spaceship Earth* in Epcot. As our "time machines" in the ride emerge to the present, we see a family watching Apollo 11 land on the moon, followed by an office housing large computers.

Narrator Judi Dench speaks of the landing on the moon by noting:

> To send a man to the moon, we had to invent a new language, spoken not by man, but by computers. At first, very large, very expensive computers, but we see the potential. What if everyone could have one of these amazing computers in their own house? There's just one problem—they're as *big* as a house! The solution comes in, of all places, a garage in California.

We then emerge into a garage scene where our narrator notes, "Young people with a passion for shaping the future put the power of the computer in everyone's hands."

Pam Fisher, Imagineer, and the show's writer, explained:

> We all looked at that scene as an homage to...the innovation
> (that) happened in garages of California. There's a lot of this
> notion of young people in Northern California (working) on
> kitchen tables, in garages, making the personal computer
> possible.

The truth is, if you ask any teams from the corporate giants, such as
Amazon or Netflix—or virtually *any* government agency, if they have
enough resources to accomplish their goals, they will respond with
an emphatic "no!" They would like more time, more people, and
more dollars in their project budgets to comfortably deliver to the
high expectations their customers (and the bosses) have of them. But,
as one executive of Google mentioned, "every breakthrough
innovation we've ever had has come from a perception that some
resource was missing, and they had to urgently improve some aspect
of the process, or they would fail."

Returning to the Bare Minimum

Curiously, years later when Michael Eisner and Frank Wells took
over the Disney organization in 1984, they chose to move animation
out of the very offices Walt had especially created for his artists back
in 1940. They were relegated to a warehouse in Glendale—a
humbling moment for the legacy team that had faltered in quality
during the seventies. But in going back to the basics they got down to
business and created a second renaissance of Disney animation
which included *The Little Mermaid, Aladdin, Beauty and the Beast* and *The
Lion King*.

Remember...there's nothing special about the garage ambiance—
but it can be the growth medium for ideas. Removing distractions
helps your mind see with a clearer, laser-like vision. Your vision of
the future—the what-could-be future—becomes keener without the
what-is present getting in the way. When it's just you (and maybe
you, too) and a blank slate of endless opportunities that are
unincumbered by any corporate vision.

Clearly, you have to provide people (including yourselves) with the resources necessary to do their job. That means the right hardware and software in terms of furnishings and tools. It also means placing them in an environment that supports the culture you want to create. Still, sometimes the best setting is the one that focuses you on what you want to accomplish, rather than supplying the comforts and luxuries that keep you distracted. Sometimes the best setting is one that makes you hungry for something better.

Ideas for the Next Century

Consider how you can make the magic come alive for you:

- For you, what are the essential *basics* for your success?

- What distractions do you need to strip *away* from your life to focus on the things that matter most?

- How can you free yourself from the encumbrances of the status quo and shift your focus to determine *your* next big thing?

3

Alice and the Lucky Rabbit

Luck Favors the Owner of Persistence

Alice Comedies

A couple of months into the new Disney Brothers Studio, the brothers rented a place in the back of a real estate office for $10 a month. When the first check arrived, they purchased their first "backlot" in the form of a vacant strip of land on Hollywood Boulevard and Rodney Drive for another $10 a month. Here they could film the live action sequences with Virginia Davis as Alice. The agreement to again start up the *Alice Comedies* was that the little girl be in the film. Walt convinced the family to bring Virginia Davis out to California and paid her $100 a month.

Additionally, Walt felt he needed a good artist in the form of Ub Iwerks, who he associated with back in Kansas City. Ub was not that excited to come out to California, but also took a role making $40 a month, the equivalent of what Walt himself was making. As production started, they eventually moved into a small store at 4649 Kingswell Avenue. The rent there was $42 which included a garage. On the store front read the words "DISNEY BROS. STUDIO."

For many months it was touch-and-go. Walt worked to improve each picture and that usually meant a smaller profit margin. The Disney brothers lived together in the same apartment. Eventually the strain of that made Roy plead with Edna to have her come out and marry him. They did so in Robert Disney's house in April of 1925.

Walt was best man at the wedding. Edna chose a woman by the name of Lillian Bounds to be the maid of honor. Through a friend, Lillian learned of a job opening at the Disney Bros. Studio as an ink and painter and applied for the job. Soon Walt and Lillian came to know each other. Walt had made a commitment to himself that he wouldn't marry until he was twenty-five and had $10,000 saved in the bank. They married on July 13, 1925, coming up short on the age commitment and woefully short on the money.

Marital commitments can do much to make someone become extremely focused on making a business succeed. Their expenses were all over the place, and about the same time that Walt married, Roy and Walt put down a payment for an office on Hyperion Avenue. In addition, there was another marital commitment that played against them. Earlier, when Margaret Winkler married Charles Mintz, she had her husband take over the contract. Soon thereafter, Mintz reported having his own business problems and started making half-payments for each film produced.

Walt put everything he could into making the best picture possible—often costing them more than what the previous film had. But audience response was positive and by December of 1924 when contract renewal came up, not only was $1800 a picture offered, but a share of the profits from rentals to theaters.

Checks were being brought in personally by Charles Mintz's brother-in-law and Hollywood representative, George Winkler, but that didn't guarantee they came in on time. They would reach out to family and others for a loan—even a former Kansas City theater organist, Carl Stalling, loaned them $275 to help them out.

It was nip-and-tuck for some time, with Mintz pointing out that they were losing money on the films. It would be the first of a long series of hard lessons Disney would have to learn working with distributors. All the creativity in the world didn't necessarily pay out. Show business was two words—tied together for better or worse. A compromise at one point was made where the brothers took only $1500 but received an increased share of 50% the profits.

Oswald the Lucky Rabbit

1926 was ending and so were the *Alice Comedies*. They simply had run their course. Carl Laemmle, founder of Universal Pictures, told Mintz he would like to see a series based on a rabbit. Walt set himself to create a character known as Oswald the Lucky Rabbit. *Poor Papa* was the first Oswald film, and management at Universal found the film sloppy and of poor quality. Too many gags and not enough story. Moreover, there was too much repetition in the animation.

All this may have been hard feedback at the time to Walt, but learning these lessons around character, story, and quality were important. Changes had to be made quickly. Agility mattered. Working late mattered, and often Walt and Ub worked late nights to get it right. A second film, *Trolley Troubles* came out of the labor they put in.

In short order, both audiences and critics responded favorably to Oswald. Even merchandise came out—though the brothers received no royalty. Still, checks for $2,250 came promptly this time around and success looked so good that the brothers bought adjoining lots and built prefabricated homes for they and their wives.

A Hard Lesson to Learn

When the contract was scheduled for renewal in February of 1928, Walt chose to take Lillian with him by train to renegotiate the contract in New York City with Mintz. They were hoping for $2500 a picture. Their time began with not only Mintz but his wife Margaret Winkler, where they had lunch at the Hotel Astor. As Bob Thomas recounts it:

> Jack Alicoate, editor of *Film Daily*, stopped at the table, and Mintz introduced him to the young producer of the Oswald cartoons. "Oswald—oh, yes," said Alicoate. "I've heard nice things about them, especially the nice grosses." Walt was

pleased, but he noticed that Mintz seemed disturbed by the remark.

Such a comment by Alicoate gave Walt the courage to ask for more money per film. But Mintz countered by going back to the $1800 figure of the *Alice* shorts. And then came the clincher: "Either you come with me at my price, or I'll take your organization away from you…I have your key men signed up."

Walt remembered Ub mentioning to him that Mintz's brother-in-law had been picking up Oswald reels and posters at night and then chatting with artists. Other than Ub, Walt had lost his animators. Walt asked Universal to intervene, but their executives sided with Mintz. Still, Walt telegrammed Roy: "…Don't worry. I really do feel that everything will turn out all right. Anyways I believe that whatever does happen is FOR THE BEST."

When an individual or organization struggles—especially at the start of something new, it's hard to gain the traction and momentum to move forward. Money is an important, if not a powerful incentive, but when that money isn't coming in the way you hoped it would, what do you lean on to keep you moving forward, especially when others are not in support of you?

As an afterthought, Mickey Mouse would be the answer to Walt's troubles. But Oswald didn't completely leave Disney permanently. In 2003, NBCUniversal was trying to obtain long-standing sportscaster Al Michaels. He had provided coverage for 30 years to include 20 years on ABC's Monday Night Football, but that show had gone to ESPN, and Michael wanted to join long-time partner John Madden on NBC. In the trade of Michaels leaving ABC and going to NBC, Disney CEO Bob Iger required that Oswald be released by Universal Studios and brought back into the Disney fold. He was immediately put to work in various ways throughout Disney from Disney+ to video games to theme park meet 'n' greets.

Ideas for the Next Century

Consider how you can make the magic come alive for you:

- Are you more than just luck?

- Can you *persist* when conditions are continually "touch-and-go"?

- What incentives or responsibilities are in place to drive you to persist?

- Are you open to receiving the feedback you need to move towards improvement?

- Do you believe that whatever happens could still turn out for the best?

Mickey Mouse Beginnings

Finding Your Hidden You

In Walt Disney's words: "I hope that we don't lose sight of one thing—that it all was started by a mouse."

Those who favor all things Disney are often known for their love of the "Hidden Mickey." They look for it in the details everywhere, from animated films to merchandise, from cruise ship lobbies to theme park queues. Many are small and are deep inside other details. At one time, one very "hidden Mickey" could only be seen from the air in an enormous covering of the entire hub in what was then Disney-MGM Studios, with Echo Lake forming the right ear.

But the *greatest* "Hidden Mickey" was inside of Walt Disney.

A New Star is Born

The story of Mickey Mouse is almost apocryphal. But there are some key elements that hold true:

- Walt learned in New York that he did not legally own the Oswald character.

- Not only did Mintz take away the rabbit, but he also took away most of his artists by having his brother-in-law negotiate deals to work for him.

23

- The idea for a character starring a mouse came on a train ride Walt and Lillian took from New York back to California.

- The original name considered was Mortimer. Lillian talked Walt out of that—so he was renamed "Mickey" Mouse. Roy and Ub agreed that Mickey was better than Mortimer.

- Before releasing Mickey, Walt had to finish out his contract with the Oswald shorts under production. This created a tension in the office working with the artists who were moving on with Mintz.

- Only Ub remained as the only animator faithful to Walt, He played a key role in making Mickey come alive.

- The initial work on Mickey Mouse occurred behind a locked door. At one point, Ub put out some 700 drawings in one day.

- The rest of the animation process happened in another garage— this time Walt's. Here drawings were inked and painted by Lillian and his niece, a daughter of his oldest brother Herbert. The images were then put under camera in the garage by other office support who had stayed faithful to Walt.

Despite all those difficult circumstances, Walt remained optimistic.

Walt left New York and went back to Hollywood to create the first Mickey Mouse short that was based on Charles Lindberg's famous nonstop, transatlantic flight. It was known as *Plane Crazy*. It was previewed in May 1928 with a good, but not strong, response. However, efforts to find a distributor interested in the project failed. Meanwhile, Walt began a second film entitled *Gallopin' Gaucho*.

Making a Sound Choice

Walt was looking for a "hook" that would set him apart from the rest. During this period, a new film premiered on October 6, 1927, that was all the rage in Hollywood: *The Jazz Singer*. It was the first talking motion picture to truly enter the marketplace. Walt was so impressed that he commenced work on a third short that would be syncopated to sound, using narrative, sound effects, and two tunes—"Steamboat Bill" and "Turkey in the Straw." He would title it, *Steamboat Willie*.

How to synchronize everything up with the film was completely new to Walt. He obtained a metronome and then timed the music to film playing on a projector at 24 frames per second. They tested it by running a projector through a window onto a bedsheet screen and then playing all of the music and FX live. Walt provided the voice of Mickey Mouse. They invited the wives to come and watch, but they really didn't pay attention.

More testing and adjusting was done, and then Walt took a silent version of the film and headed to New York to have it recorded. He stopped in Kansas City on the way to visit a theater organist friend, Carl Stalling, who composed a musical score for the film.

Walt shopped the Big Apple for someone to do the work needed. They were either unavailable, too expensive, or lacked good technology. Some tried to persuade him to simply put the sound on a record and play it alongside the film. Walt befriended a man by the name of Pat Powers, who seemed connected to everyone. He helped arrange the recording sessions and offered his own recording system called Cinephone. But Walt knew that system had problems and would not guarantee the synch necessary. He notes:

> …I have come to this definite conclusion: Sound effects and talking pictures are more than a mere novelty. They are here to stay and in time will develop into a wonderful thing. The ones that get in on the ground floor are the ones that will most likely profit by its future development. That is, providing they work for quality and not quantity and quick money. Also, I am convinced that the sound on film is the only logical thing for the future. At the present it is necessary to have both in order to cover the field one hundred percent.

Two expensive efforts to record the soundtrack of the movie resulted in a finished product and Roy having to sell Walt's beloved Moon roadster. Walt peddled the film around New York to a very uncertain reception. Whatever anxiety and uncertainty he carried in Manhattan was presented differently in letters: "All together now— 'Are we downhearted? HELL NO.'" The HELL NO was typed in red.

Finding an Audience

One man, Harry Reichenbach, saw the short in a screening operated by the Colony Theater in New York for Universal Pictures. He offered to show it. Walt was uncertain as it was a Broadway theater, not a movie house. But Reichenbach insisted that until audiences saw it and clamored for more, there would be no response from distributors. In addition, he offered Walt $500 a week to run the short. That was a huge amount of money needed to address their financial shortfalls.

Steamboat Willie opened at the Colony Theater on November 18th, 1928. Reichenbach was right. Not only were audience members clamoring, so were the critics. Even the New York Times shared that it was "an ingenious piece of work with a good deal of fun. It growls, whines, squeaks, and makes various other sounds that add to its mirthful quality."

Among the many distributors who came a-calling was Universal— with Charles Mintz eager to set up a deal. Walt was professional but declined any offer. Pat Powers came around and said he would sell the film around the country, take care of expenses, and only keep 10% of the grosses. Walt thought the deal was great and came back home to Roy in California with $2500. Then Roy read the contract— which Walt had not studied. They owed Pat Powers $26,000 a year for the next ten years for the use of a Cinephone to record the short.

Still, by the time Walt returned to New York City, the popularity of Mickey Mouse was well underway. In 1929, it became a craze all over the country, with theaters starting up Mickey Mouse Clubs in the theaters. Even a catch phrase—and subsequent song by Irving

Cesar—"What! No Mickey Mouse?" came into vogue when moviegoers realized no Mickey Mouse short was showing. To this day, Mickey's appeal universally has made him the most recognized drawn character icon in the world.

The Real "Hidden Mickey"

Returning to those early moments when Walt's idea for Mickey Mouse was nothing but a few drawings, he showed them to Ub Iwerks after getting off the train and returning to his studio in California. Studying the sketches, Ub noted: "looks exactly like you—same nose, same face, same whiskers, same gestures, and expressions. All he needs now is your voice". In truth the most "Hidden Mickey" of them all is Walt Disney himself. He was the first "Hidden Mickey."

Walt Disney said: "I hope that we never lose sight of one thing, that it was all started by a mouse.

Julie Andrews in "One Man's Dream" shares that same quote then responds, "but we know that it really was all started by a man, a man with a dream…and a mouse."

Ideas for the Next Century

Consider how you can make the magic come alive for you:

- What is the Hidden Mickey inside of you? What are the qualities you possess that can make your dreams come true?

- What are the obstacles that keep you from making your dreams come true?

- How do you fight against or keep from caving in to those obstacles?

- How often will you need to start over to make a dream come true?

- What is your response to rejection? How do you make a comeback?

- Who can you partner with to make your dreams come true?

- Do the criticisms of others drag you down or make you even more determined to succeed?

5

Silly Symphonies

A Silly Approach to a Serious Need

Mickey Mouse was not just a likeable, enjoyable cartoon character. The technology that made the mouse stand out from the rest was a formula for being a leader in a crowded market of cartoon creations. But for Walt to truly make a sustainable break, he would need to continue to drive new characters, new stories, and new improvements in the work he was doing.

Successful But Broke

Before Walt and Roy could move forward, they needed a new distributor, as it was becoming all too clear that Pat Powers could not be trusted. Roy exclaimed:

> Look, Walt, we have to face the situation. Here we are, owners of the most famous cartoon character in the United States—in the world, maybe—with crowds lining up to see him in movie houses from Anchorage to Buenos Aires, and we're flat broke! We don't have enough money in the bank to finance the next series, and I'm not sure whether they're going to let us have the credit. I think Pat Powers is screwing us!

To that end, Roy went to New York on the next trip and came back to Walt decidedly certain that things needed changing. So, Walt went back to the Big Apple with not only Lillian, but with a colorful attorney, Gunther Lessing, a man who had provided legal representation to Pancho Villa during the Mexican Revolution. Walt and Roy would get out of that obligation, but it cost them money—in particular taking back the pictures they had released like *Steamboat Willie*.

The good news is now Mickey Mouse was clearly successful, and distributors were more than interested in meeting with him. On the recommendation of acclaimed director Frank Capra, they worked for a short time with Columbia Pictures. But that, too, had problems. So not long afterwards, they found a fairer deal with United Artists (UA). UA was founded by artists like Mary Pickford, Douglas Fairbanks, Samuel Goldwyn, and Charlie Chaplin, for whom Walt had a particular fondness. It turned out that Charlie Chaplin loved Mickey Mouse! In Bob Thomas's biography of Walt Disney, Chaplin shared with Walt: "You're going to develop more; you're getting ahold of your medium…But to protect your independence, you've got to do as I have done—own every picture you make." Walt was thrilled with the prospect, and it gave him freedom to create new characters, new stories, and new technologies.

New Characters

With *Steamboat Willie*, the world had been introduced not just to Mickey Mouse, but Minnie Mouse and Pegleg Pete. In future shorts they would be introduced to crazy characters like Pluto, Goofy, and Donald Duck. Donald was introduced in a *Silly Symphony* short known as *The Wise Little Hen*. This vehicle led him to become a breakout character. It allowed Walt to do things with story and character he couldn't quite do with his first star, Mickey. Crowds loved Donald and in time more shorts were built around him than Mickey himself. Other characters emerged as well through *The Silly Symphony* films such as *Little Hiawatha*, *The Ugly Duckling*, and *The Three Little Pigs*.

New Stories

Still, a world of stories made of cartoon animals was not enough for Walt either. He needed to play with other stories, other themes. He knew that "same old" could not consistently play in the bijou. So, Walt began a series of films entitled, *The Silly Symphony* series. A *Silly Symphony* short allowed any number of themes and stories to play out. There were no limits. On one occasion Walt stated "Story…must be considered the heart of the business." He continued, "Good animators can make a good story a knockout. There is not much that the best animators can do with bad stories."

Skeleton Dance was the first of these. The same Kansas City organist, Carl Stalling, who had scored *Steamboat Willie* and had loaned the brothers money suggested a film animated to Grieg's "March of the Dwarfs." But it wouldn't be dwarfs—that's later in the story—rather he was suggesting skeletons dancing in and out of graveyards. No narrative, just a whimsical score set to a moonlit setting. It allowed Walt to test certain production techniques.

New Technology

That same curiosity was furthered as Disney ventured into utilizing technology in new ways that would improve the cinematic experience. Here are some examples:

Flowers & Trees: Utilizing music from Mendelssohn and Schubert, Walt was already halfway done with the film in black and white when he approached the Technicolor organization. Roy was concerned with the costs of color and its reliability. Walt used that concern to get Technicolor to give Disney exclusivity on the three-color process for the first two years to assure other cartoon companies couldn't rush in and do the same. After a premiere at Grauman's Chinese Theater, bookings were as much in demand as Mickey Mouse.

Santa's Workshop: This was the first cartoon to employ optical sound. Moving away from earlier sound recording efforts, this was the technology that placed the soundtrack on the side of the film print as it went through the projector. Walt would use that abstract celluloid printed image to come alive in *Fantasia* later as a character that separated itself from the film strip.

The Old Mill: This film employed what became known as the multiplane camera. This in-house creation was a large vertical camera set up with different layers of cells to be spaced apart at different distances while allowing lighting to be adjusted to each layer. The camera looked down on all of this as both it and the cells were adjusted vertically. This allowed for greater depth of motion. It was as if the objects rendered before the camera were in three dimensions. Added to this were new special FX touches to include rain, lightning, fire, ripples of water, and reflective surfaces. The cumulative effect was one that gave animation much more of a sense of realism far different than that of simple cartoons a decade earlier.

The word "silly" can be defined as lacking common sense or judgement. It describes something that can't be taken seriously. While the themes of these cartoons were indeed silly, Walt's approach to this medium was anything but silly. He took seriously the idea that making improvements was the path toward success. Indeed, *The Silly Symphony* series was his path toward preparing not only the studio but the theatrical audience for a more serious work: *Snow White and the Seven Dwarfs.* Through new stories, beloved characters, and improved technologies, Walt made serious improvement through *The Silly Symphony* series.

Because Walt was serious not silly, he won his first Oscar in 1932 for *Flowers & Trees,* and via *The Silly Symphony* series, won the Oscar every year from that year through 1939, winning more Oscars than any other cartoon series. Additionally, he received an Honorary Academy Award that first year for the creation of Mickey Mouse. In time he would hold the record for the most Academy Awards received—a total of twenty-six to include honorary awards. He also received a total of fifty-nine nominations, not only making him hold the distinction of having won the most Oscars, but also having more nominations than any other figure in the cinematic world.

Ideas for the Next Century

Consider how you can make the magic come alive for you:

- How serious are you about making improvements to your field of endeavor?

- For Walt, it was about improving stories, characters, and technology. What are the critical things you need to work on improving?

- How can those improvements help you to stand out in your own field or industry?

6

Who's Afraid of the Big Bad Wolf?

The Best House of Bricks Is Mentally Tough

October 29, 1929, was nothing Hollywood could have ever dreamed up. Known as Black Tuesday, stock prices collapsed, and more than 16 million shares were traded on the New York Stock Exchange in a single day. Billions of dollars were lost, and in the following months and years a Great Depression ensued. By 1933, nearly half of America's banks had gone under, and nearly 30% of America was unemployed.

The Long Night of Depression

Walt and Roy had invested in their own company, not in the stock market. That investment was keeping them alive. But to make it work they had to grind out more shorts—and all for less money. This day-in, day-out approach took a toll on Walt. For the sake of getting through hard times, it was difficult to bring creativity and innovation to bear. George Morris noted to one reporter, "His hobby is his work…as every moment of his time is given to it." Lillian tried to use humor in an interview with Time magazine when she labeled herself as a "mouse widow." But she also confided that at night Walt "would usually toss and turn, thinking of studio problems, then rise early and declare, 'I think I've got it licked.'"

That sort of day-in, day-out focus eventually led Walt to a nervous breakdown. It seemed that with every success came the threat of struggle, even insolvency. He became difficult to work with at the office, sometimes failing to focus and drawing a blank, other times ripping into employees over the work they had done. This downward spiral led to the doctor advising him to get away and take a needed rest.

Keeping the Wolves of Life Away

The initial thought was to take Lillian on a sort of second honeymoon by sailing down the Mississippi river. But when they got to St. Louis, they learned that the passenger trade for such voyages had been drained by the Depression. (He would remedy that in years to come with his own river boat on his own Mississippi-like river). Changing plans they took a train to Washington, D.C., saw the sights, then headed south on another train to Key West, Florida, where they boarded a cruise ship for Cuba, through the Panama Canal, and then back up again to Los Angeles.

Returning relaxed, he bought a membership at the Hollywood Athletic Club, exercising early in the morning, or would play golf at nearby Griffith Park. In time he would join a polo club, playing with the likes of Will Rogers, Spencer Tracy, and Darryl F. Zanuck. He enjoyed the networking that came with the sport, though he would complain of ailments for years to come due to playing polo.

These would be the mechanisms that helped Walt get through these uncertain years. On the home front, he and Lillian built a new home in 1933, and then at the end of the year, welcomed their first daughter, Diane Marie Disney, into the family. A few years later Sharon Mae Disney would join the family. Over time, Walt withdrew more from the social life of Hollywood to spend more time with his small growing family. In part, this withdrawal may have been influenced by the "crime of the century"—the kidnapping of Charles Lindberg's 20-month-old son. Perhaps the creator of children and family entertainment needed to keep a lower profile.

Building a Better House

The bottom line was that these were uncertain times. Roy Disney spoke of that time and his own fears:

> When the banks were closed in 1933, of course I was frantic—what are we gonna do for money? So, I was stewing and worrying, and Walt was impatient with me. He said, "Quit worrying about it. People aren't going to stop living just because the banks are closed. What the hell, we'll make potatoes the medium of exchange. We'll pay everybody in potatoes.

Clearly facing tough times and finding ways to cope with those difficulties gave Walt a better paradigm of the world he was in. To that end he offered an answer to a very scared country in the form of a short, *The Three Little Pigs*, released on May 27, 1933. While other *Silly Symphony* shorts usually made some $50K in the box office over its initial year, this film made over 150K in the first fifteen months. It won the Academy Award that year for Best Animated Short Film, and it has since been selected for preservation in the United States National Film Registry by the Library of Congress for its cultural and historical significance.

To make this short really stand out, Walt needed a song. A simple tune as easy to remember as "Happy Birthday" would provide a rallying cry. Frank Churchill's tune "Who's Afraid of the Big Bad Wolf" became such a theme for people embroiled in the depths of the Depression. (Churchill would later write the songs for *Snow White and the Seven Dwarfs*.) His "Big Bad Wolf" lyrics speak of working through one's fears and difficulties by focusing on hard work and effort. Changing the original tale, even the pigs who built houses of straw and sticks were able to escape their fate, rather than be consumed by the wolf. To Walt, the story was simple: Build a foundation as strong as brick and mortar rather than one of straw and stick so you can endure whatever comes along. Or in other words, hope and possibility favors the prepared. As Walt Disney later noted:

People sort of live in the dark about things. A lot of young people think the future is closed to them, that everything has been done. This is not so. There are still plenty of avenues to be explored.... For youngsters of today, I say: believe in the future, the world is getting better, there is still plenty of opportunity.

The Three Little Pigs ran for months in the theaters, and Walt capitalized on its success by creating additional pig-and-wolf shorts. Still, in the end, he realized that "you can't top pigs with pigs." It was at this time that Walt envisioned something much bigger, a full-length feature film. But he would need a more talented team to make that happen. He would need a house of bricks, not one of sticks. One that was mentally prepared to take on such an endeavor.

Ideas for the Next Century

Consider how you can make the magic come alive for you:

- How do you seek to defeat the bad wolves that come along in life?

- Like the three little pigs, how is your preparation one with a solid foundation rather than one fixed on sticks and hay?

- How is doing the same thing again and again keeping you from doing something much greater?

- How are you positioning yourself to see a future of possibility and opportunity?

7

Mickey Mouse Watch

The Timing of Success

One of the definitive icons of the Walt Disney Company is the Mickey Mouse Watch. This timepiece is as much about timing as it is about time.

Time for New Income

As the depression loomed, Walt Disney was looking for new revenue sources on top of the *Mickey Mouse* and *Silly Symphony* shorts. The thought was that licensing Mickey Mouse to merchandise might be an answer to that. Herman "Kay" Kamen was an advertising man from Kansas City, and he thought he could sell Mickey Mouse in a new and better way than what was being done at the time. Kay headed to California on a train to meet with Walt. A contract soon followed which allowed Kay to be the company's sole licensing representative.

While President Herbert Hoover promised a chicken in every pot, Kay Kamen promised a Disney character in every home. Within three years, the different kinds of Mickey Mouse products numbered in the thousands. But one product uniquely stood out. During this same time, Ingersoll-Waterbury Clock Company was facing bankruptcy. Kay struck up a deal with the fledgling company to sell watches priced at $3.25. Again, timing was everything. The watches were a massive hit. Macy's department store in New York City sold a

38

record 11,000 watches in one day. The Ingersoll-Waterbury Clock Company had to increase the number of its factory workers from 300 to 3,000. In an era such as this one, *timing* couldn't have been better.

In another instance, the Lionel Corporation, that created toy electric trains, was facing bankruptcy as a result of the Depression. Kamen made an agreement to create a Mickey and Minnie wind-up handcar with a circle track that would retail for $1. In four months' time, 253,000 of the handcars were sold. It brought Lionel out of bankruptcy proceedings and made it solvent.

A Whole New Market

The rest is history. A new industry came about focusing on merchandise related to films. Disney products in that early era provided the fuel to help Walt's studio develop its first animated feature, *Snow White and the Seven Dwarfs*. Before the show's opening, Kay had some 117 manufacturers licensed to sell products from the film. He also introduced another first in merchandising—the soundtrack album. Of course, Disney products are everywhere today. Hundreds of Disney stores are scattered across the United States and abroad. Theme parks sell merchandise at the exit to nearly every attraction and park. Major properties include not just Mickey and Minnie, but *Star Wars*, *Frozen*, Disney Princess, *Cars*, *Spider-Man*, *Avengers*, *Winnie the Pooh*, and other Disney classics.

As the 1930's ended and as international markets were shutting down due to World War II, Disney merchandise royalties outweighed revenue from film rentals. In truth, managing time is about being at the right place at the right time. Almost. Just a day after having dinner in Paris with Walt and Roy, Kay and his wife died in an Air France crash over the Azores on October 27, 1940. From there, Walt and Roy would take over the business of merchandising. Occurring simultaneously, a film division was being created by the studio and a music-publishing division was being set up by the company as well—the organization soon became more attuned to the title Walt Disney Productions than it did to the animated artistry of Walt Disney.

Ideas for the Next Century

Consider how you can make the magic come alive for you:

- How can you broaden your potential?

- How is your timing with making things happen?

- How do you organize in a scramble to meet tight deadlines?

- Are there new markets you might be missing?

- What are you doing to not be late to the market?

8

Disney's Hyperion Studio

A Culture of "Family" Embracing Excellence

24 Frames a Second

To understand how different and unique the experience was working at Disney, one must begin with the simple premise—what it takes to create animation on film. It takes 24 frames or sets of images a second to fill a movie screen. At Disney, that means there must be 24 unique sets of images. Those images are first storyboarded. Then they are sketched. The sketch is finessed into a perfect drawing. The drawing is traced with ink onto a piece of celluloid. The celluloid is then painted. Backgrounds and other layers of the film that complete the picture are also drawn and painted. From there it is filmed and edited, with narrative, music, and FX added.

This is the grinding—even somewhat industrial—process that creates an animated image on the screen. It takes weeks to do a minute of film, months to make a cartoon short, and years to do a full-length feature. There are ways that you can short cut all this. But if you want to stand out in the marketplace, you must make every frame image work. Every frame must be a near-perfect piece of art.

One Mickey. Many Artists. One Family

To make animation happen requires artists. Artists are particularly unique in their style, interpretation, and expression. The trick is to get hundreds of artists to agree on how a particular character or image will be shared on the screen. They must forsake their own ego—how they think it might best look or how they might interpret it—for the collective whole. In any industry, people have an opinion. But getting artists in sync—and pointed in one direction—to do that when they define themselves by their artistic expression—is especially difficult.

So, what made the studios unique? What was the thing that separated it from all others? It was not the physical facility per se. Disney's Hyperion Studio was a sprawling set of buildings that grew over time as the needs of the fledgling studio grew. It worked fine for creating shorts, but it would burst out the doors to eventually build its first full-length feature, *Snow White and the Seven Dwarfs*. But many of the original studio pioneers had their start there, and for many of them, it was like family. That was the way they typically expressed the culture of culture of the organization.

Curiously, most successful organizations consist of employees who feel like they work for a "family." They will reference a great work experience as "we were like family." They talk about everyone knowing each other, everyone working together, everyone focusing on the same goal or outcome. Likewise, many people reference leaving an organization as "it used to feel like family, but it doesn't any more. It's not the same."

What was the experience at the Hyperion Studio that for many felt "like family"? There are many things that add to this, but perhaps these two critical components should be addressed here:

A Flattened Organization

Many reference that it was more "all hands-on deck." In this sense, you did what it took to make deadlines happen. One important aspect was that Walt insisted the organization be on a first-name basis. There were titles and organizational charts, but Walt wanted everyone to feel like they could talk to him, and most importantly, that he didn't have to go through others to talk to any one individual. Even today Cast Members in the parks where name tags with first names only.

Frank Thomas and Ollie Johnston, two of Disney's top animators wrote in *Disney Animation: The Illusion of Life* that Walt built a loosely unified group of talented people who could work together in constantly changing patterns. "What Walt wanted was the greatest creative effort—not the most efficient operation. There were titles and departments and job classifications without end, but they had more to do with responsibility than with authority."

Ideally at work, Walt wanted that collegiality in brainstorming and shaping a story or cartoon. Turning to one reporter he noted, "We voice our opinions and sometimes we have good old-fashioned scraps, but in the end, things get ironed out and we have something we're all proud of."

It wasn't perfectly that way, and in the end, everyone knew that Walt's word was final. But in Walt's mind and heart, he knew his success was getting everyone to buy in. At one point he invited artists to come up with gags. Ward Kimball talked about earning an extra $5 at that time by coming up with the gag of the 7 dwarfs popping their noses individually over each of the beds as they spied on *Snow White*. Again, it wasn't perfect, but the idea was to flatten the organization so that each could contribute. Even in the early days most of the employees had a key to the door of the studio—just like the people in your own household.

Add to this a collegial atmosphere, where animators would play pranks on each other—pouring water on a chair as someone was about to sit in it, putting cheese on the light under a colleague's animation board, or adding art gum eraser shavings in one's pipe tobacco. Roy Williams, who became the "big" Mouseketeer years later on the *Mickey Mouse Club*, was notorious for playing pranks. All of this combined to foster a sense of family. After work and weekends, the organization could be found across the street playing ball—like a family.

Embracing Excellence

There was also another aspect that added to the feeling of being part of a family. It also helps to explain how artists with such different styles and approaches could come together as one. Organizations become stronger when their individual members sacrifice and give their all. At The Walt Disney Studios everyone sacrificed and contributed to a common cause of creating and delivering animation better than anywhere else. Competing against the other animation studios and creating entertaining and highly acclaimed work was a powerful elixir for everyone who got on board. This brought people together in a powerful way.

There is a story in Christopher Hench's *The Art of Walt Disney* about Dick Huemer meeting Ben Sharpsteen on the street one day. Dick was with Charles Mintz at the time and could see that Disney had separated himself from the pack of other cartoonists. Dick wondered what the secret formula was over at Disney. He noted:

> Whenever we met a guy like Ted Sears or Ben Sharpsteen, we'd say, 'Oh, come on now—what is it that Walt does that we don't do?' and they would simply say something like, 'He analyzes.' Analyzes! So do we—we think! But we didn't and Walt did. He did chew everything over, did prepare beautifully, so the director could just take it and give it to the animator and then look at it and correct it.

Neal Gabler in *Walt Disney: The Triumph of the American Imagination* stated it well when he noted:

> The biggest difference, however, between the Disney studio and the animation studios in New York was not in preparation or specialization; it was in expectation. Walt Disney had to be the best. As he had with the *Alices* and the *Oswalds*, though with different results, Walt insisted upon excellence.

According to director Ben Sharpsteen, who in many ways was Walt's right-hand man when it came to getting these pictures made, "In Walt's estimation, everything that was done had to be executed with a great deal of thought toward finesse in order to make it better."

Gabler went on to say:

> Part of Walt's secret was that in insisting on quality from individuals of whom it had never been required, he inspired commitment. 'We'd hate to go home at night,' Iwerks recalled, 'and we couldn't wait to get to the office in the morning. We had lots of vitality, and we had to work it off.'

If excellence was the calling card for bringing together people in a unified purpose, then Walt had just the vehicle for making the studio rise above all others. Of course, it would be necessary to build that staff so they could deliver it. Many Disney veterans had their starts during these early years; together they shared the experience of just trying to figure out how to deliver improved animation, especially when resources were limited and unavailable. But Walt had a vision of something that would define their ability to deliver something that no other studio had ever come close to creating—a full-length animated film.

Ideas for the Next Century

Consider how you can make the magic come alive for you:

- What mundane aspects of your work must you get others to rise above?

- What makes your organization feel like "family" working together?

- What common cause brings you together and unites you as one?

- How does sacrifice bring your "family" together?

- What are your expectations around excellence?

9

Moving from Cartoon Shorts to a Full-Length Animated Feature

Having the Vision & Talent

With a "family" of artists supporting Walt in creating the greatest animation studio ever, it was now possible to elevate the art of animation to another level. Walt had a vision of what that could be. It was a vision of something much bigger than cartoon shorts. It would be about creating an animated art form that would be the reason why guests would come to the theater.

The Vision

This vision had come to Walt over the years, even as early as the time he commenced work. While a young news boy in Kansas City, he was able to catch a 1916 film starring Marguerite Clark in the role of Snow White. The experience made an impression. Years later he and Roy came to London to receive a medal from the League of Nations for Mickey Mouse. During a tour of Paris, they found a theater playing six Mickey Mouse shorts back-to-back and nothing else. Clearly audiences would sit through an animated feature. But the best evidence of building out a film of this caliber came in their own bank accounts. As long as they were the introductory short and not the feature, they would continue struggling with making ends meet. Walt knew the big money would come from being the marquee header. He also knew it would take big money to make big money.

One evening early in 1934, Walt Disney gave everyone 65 cents to go get a bite to eat at a café across from the Hyperion Studio. When they returned he invited them to the studio's empty sound stage, sat them down and, in Ken Anderson's words, "proceeded to intrigue us from eight o'clock until early midnight acting and telling [the story of Snow White] even anticipating the songs and the kind of music, and he so thrilled us with the complete recitation of all the characters that he had created that we were just carried away…we had no concept that we were ever going to do anything else or want to do anything else. We wanted to do what he had just told us!"

The Talent

To make that vision a reality, Walt needed quantity and quality. He needed an enormous and talented team to accomplish the work of creating *Snow White*. Walt always believed in developing his staff. In the early days of animation, he was concerned about his animators' ability to draw human figures and make them appear natural in their movements. As early as 1931, Walt was paying for artists to attend evening classes at Chouinard Art School in Los Angeles. The following year, Walt invited Donald Graham to start an art-training program at the Hyperion studio, with the goal of recruiting no fewer than 300 new artists. Graham himself recalled:

> From eight in the morning till nine at night, what was probably the most unique art school in the world was conducted. As *Snow White* began to take shape, various experts from all branches of the studio were called upon to contribute to the program. Intensive lectures on character construction, animation, layout, background, mechanics, and direction extended studio knowledge to the youngest neophyte.

Space was found across the studio for this art school. Added to this more formal training were the following:

- Walt came back from his trip to Europe with a wide range of children's illustrated books, which were made available to artists to study.
- Artists would see ballets and a variety of films. In particular, they would rush to see their own works play out before audiences. And then they would huddle afterwards while the main film played to critique what worked and what didn't.
- Some artists had strong artistic skills, but little sense of showmanship, entertainment, or even the delivery of a gag. Those needs required training as well.

Finally, these skills had to be tried and tested out. The Silly Symphony episodes such as *Music Land* and *Who Killed Cock Robin?* along with new Mickey shorts like *The Band Concert* and *Thru the Mirror* were evidence of such improved efforts.

Learning the real *art* of animation was a shared set of experiences they came to experience. With that, the studio geared up for an intense effort to build the first full-length animated film, *Snow White and the Seven Dwarfs*. Story teams were put in place, talented artists were assigned to key characters in the film, and the entire organization put its momentum toward creating this first full-length animated feature.

Ideas for the Next Century

Consider how you can make the magic come alive for you:

- What is your vision for taking you and those around you forward?

- Are you able to articulate that vision in a way that gets others onboard?

- What value is an education to fulfilling your dreams?

- How important is it that you develop others?

10

Disney's Folly: Snow White and the Seven Dwarfs

Defying the Expectations of Others

Richard Holliss and Brian Sibley's *Snow White and the Seven Dwarfs & the Making of the Classic Film* includes this story of what Walt encountered upon his first journey to Los Angeles:

> I [Walt] met a guy on the train when I was comin' out. It was one of those things that kind of made you mad. I was on the back platform—I was in my pants and coat that didn't match but I was riding first class. I was making conversation with a guy who asked me, "Goin' to California?"
>
> "Yea, I'm goin' out there." "What business you in?"
>
> I said, "The motion-picture business."
>
> Then, all of a sudden, "Oh, is that right? Well, I know somebody in the picture business. What do you do?"
>
> I said, "I make animated cartoons." "Oh."
>
> It was like saying, "I sweep up the latrines."

It is conceivable that this conversation played into Walt for several years to come. Certainly, diminishing returns and the limits of creating just shorts was on his mind. So, when we went toward building a film that would be a full-length feature and not just an opening act for one, he was determined to make something that would be respected and revered—even by the guy he met on the train.

The Folly

Walt sunk his total resources into *Snow White*. Just consider all that Walt had to deal with to bring *Snow White and the Seven Dwarfs* to the screen:

- No one had ever really done a full-length animated feature before. Max Fleischer had attempted a five and a half reel in 1926 called *Theory of Relativity*, but it was not at a level to compete with a complete feature film.
- Walt's animators had to become experts at drawing humans, not just simply creating cartoons. Animals in the film had to look less cartoony.
- Parents and critics were concerned that looking at something for so long in color would hurt their children's eyes. Colors would need to be muted or showcased more in pastels.
- Early attempts at writing the music for the film were met with resistance. Walt wanted a song to weave into the story, not have the performers burst into song.
- The Hyperion Studio didn't have enough space for all the artists needed to work on the film. People were spread out in adjoining buildings.
- The scale of the drawings themselves made it difficult for Snow White to appear with all the animals at one time, or with all the dwarfs. Not only were larger drawings required, but animation boards, sliding cel boards, checking boards, and inking-painting boards had to be re-designed. Cameras had to be adapted as well.

- The distributor thought Walt should down-play the idea that *Snow White* was a fairy tale "because audiences don't buy fairy tales." The distributor wanted to sell it as a romantic tale. Those differences would result in Disney changing the distributor to RKO.
- Recouping the costs would come at 18 cents a ticket because that was the going rate to see a movie in 1937.

Because of all of this, people began to doubt. At one point, Walt was so concerned about the negative word on the street that he asked the advice of United Artists' distribution manager: "What should I do about all the bad talk about the feature?" The reply? "Nothing. Keep them wondering. Let 'em call it Disney's folly or any other damn thing, as long as they keep talking about it. That picture is going to pay off, and the more suspense you build up, the more it will pay off."

No place was the suspense more palpable than with the bank. As more and more money was being requested, the Bank of America grew weary, and expressed the need for reassurance. Roy told Walt that he needed to show what he had. Walt was hugely resistant, as he only had bits and pieces. Parts were in color. Other segments were pencil animation. And the rest was in static layout sketches.

Walt gave in and hosted bank officer Joseph Rosenberg for a first screening of the film. Walt had to fill in lines of dialogue and action to provide a sense of continuity. Rosenberg sat through all of this as Walt reassured him of his vision. The lights came up at the end and Rosenberg said little as he headed out to his car. As he departed, Rosenberg thanked Walt for his time, said goodbye, and closed the door of his car. As an afterthought, he called out: "That thing is going to make you a hatful of money." With that, Rosenberg drove off and Walt got the monies necessary to finish the film.

The Result

Some 30,000 patrons mobbed the entrance to the Carthay Circle Theater the night of Tuesday, December 21, 1937. Staff as well as celebrities like Ginger Rogers, Charlie Chaplin, and Shirley Temple walked along the red carpet and into the theaters. Inside the lights darkened, the music went up, and the film came to life before its invited guests: The credits read as follows:

A Walt Disney Feature Production
Snow White and the Seven Dwarfs

Following initial credits an expression of gratitude came on the screen,

"My sincere appreciation to the members of my staff whose loyalty and creative endeavor made possible this production." Walt Disney

Animator Shamus Culhane wrote:

> It was the most receptive, enthusiastic audience I have ever seen. Every song, every gag, every good piece of acting worked on those people like a bow on a fiddle. There was almost continuous laughter and applause until Frank Thomas' sequence, where the sorrowing dwarfs gather around Snow White's bier. The house fell silent, gripped by the emotional impact of the acting. It was the first-time grief had been so dramatically depicted in an animated film.

In the end, Walt's vision came true, and the film garnered rave reviews and grossed $8 million worldwide. It was a bright moment in a time when people were trying to pull out of a long depression.

Returning to that conversation on the train when Walt came to California in 1923, he noted:

> Some people make you mad, and you want to prove something to them even though they mean nothing to you. I thought of that guy... when we had the premiere of *Snow White*. And the darn thing went out and grossed eight million dollars around the world.

53

Ideas for the Next Century

Consider how you can make the magic come alive for you:

- How do the attitudes or impressions of others instigate a desire toward change?

- How do you face the follies others see in your efforts?

- How do you persist when others expect you to fail?

11

The Golden Age of Hollywood

A Tale of Two Leadership Styles

A Golden Age of Animation

The 1930s and into 1940s was the Golden Age of Hollywood—certainly such was the case for The Walt Disney Studios. Even *before* the premiere of *Snow White and the Seven Dwarfs* at the Carthay Circle Theater in 1937, the studio was beginning to create some of the most beautiful and distinctive full-length feature films ever released:

1940: *Pinocchio*. Perhaps the greatest film in terms of artistic craftsmanship. "When You Wish Upon a Star" became a signature anthem for the studio.

1940: *Fantasia*. An anthology of shorts threaded together by classical music and an enormous departure from *The Silly Symphony* experience. Like *The Silly Symphony* series, it used an extraordinary, but unsuccessful, concept called Fantasound. This was a sound reproduction system generating a pioneering stereophonic sound. It was only employed by 13 theaters in major markets due to its expensive cost.

1941: *Dumbo*. Made on a shoestring compared to the previous three films, it had heart and soul—though made on the premise that less is more.

1942: *Bambi.* A circle-of-life film with emotional moments that stretch as far as the forest it depicts.

Two Studios—Two Worlds

The studios became a factory for great artistry, but it was still the smallest game in town. The biggest was the infamous MGM (Metro Goldwyn Mayer) Studios headed by Louis B. Mayer. From the end of the silent film era through World War II, MGM was known as having "more stars than there are in heaven," a reference to the large number of famous movie stars under contract to the studio.

At the other end of the spectrum from MGM back in the 30s and 40s was "the little studio that could": Walt Disney Productions. A study of Disney and Mayer's approaches as studio heads offers important insights into what makes a successful positional leader.

So great was this distinction that even decades later, the third theme park established at Walt Disney World in 1989 was originally called Disney-MGM Studios. To that end, the entrance arch featured both Mickey Mouse and MGM's Leo the Lion. As the park was built, Michael Eisner thought the Disney name would not be enough to bring in tourists who wanted to visit a working studio. Eisner wanted to link it with a bigger name. Cleverly, they gained the rights to use the MGM name for a bargain during the development of the new park in the 1980s. To understand the difference between these two studios during this pivotal time is to understand the two individuals who headed up those studios.

Louis B. Mayer's Leadership Approach

In the film attraction, *Golden Dreams*, Louis B. Mayer, the head of MGM, shares: "My philosophy is quite simple. I hire the best people. Then I give them plenty of freedom to do their best. And if I don't like their best work, I fire them!"

This philosophy is known as "bring me a rock." It's a frequently played-out tactic among demanding managers. If your rock is presentable, great. But if it isn't, you're expected to bring a new "rock" in a short time frame. Little if any criteria or understanding is provided. You're simply expected to bring the right rock. It's all capricious. And if you don't deliver, you're often demeaned, disciplined, or even fired. "Give me more musicals." "Put Bogart under contract." MGM Studios survived because it kept bringing more "rocks" to the theater—no matter what it took.

That philosophy did pay off in many ways. Some of the most beloved movies were created through this studio system, including *The Wizard of Oz*, *Singing in the Rain*, and *Gone with the Wind*. At one time, Mayer was the highest paid man in the country, and stars like Robert Taylor and Greer Garson viewed him as a father figure. But others, like Elizabeth Taylor, described him as a monster to deal with. Scott Eyman, in his biography of Louis B. Mayer, shared what the acclaimed actress Helen Hayes noted:

> You are talking the devil incarnate. Not just evil, but the most evil man I have ever dealt with in my life. He was an untalented, mean, vicious, vindictive person. He deliberately undermined people, went after individuals who were good box office for Loew's, Inc.: Buster Keaton, Billy Haines. He turned everyone against everyone else, establishing himself as a kingpin, without having anything to offer himself. And he would lie to your face.

Mayer's role to was demand perfection of others no matter what. That approach yielded results, but at a cost. Samuel Goldwyn stated: "The only reason so many people attended his funeral was they wanted to make sure he was dead."

Walt Disney's Leadership Approach

A child once asked Walt Disney, "Do you draw Mickey Mouse?" His confession was that he had long left that task to his illustrators. The child then asked, "Well, what do you do?"

Walt told this youngster that he was like a little bee, going from flower to flower providing pollen so that things could grow. Walt's philosophy was to develop and nurture others in order to meet the vision of what he needed to create. Peter Ellenshaw, a studio artist, explained it this way:

> He'd fill you with fire. I always tried to understand how he made me feel so good. It was magical, really. He said one time he was 'the bee that pollinated the flowers', but he didn't do it in a way you might think, like, "Oh, Peter, this is coming great. Oooh! Very good!" He'd never say anything like that. He'd talk about the project rather than how good or bad you were doing. He inspired you to create what *he* wanted.

Reports that Walt built a tightly run organization were inaccurate. Such a structure never really existed, according to Frank Thomas and Ollie Johnston. They pointed out that this was no ordinary organization but one run under the direction of the man Walt Disney. His direction as the leader of the company came not because he had final say, but because he brought creative leadership to the table.

> This method worked because Walt was the boss—not just because it was his studio or that he had authority to get what he wanted, but because his ideas were best. Many times, we could not understand what he wanted, but never did we lose confidence in him or his ability. We could question his judgement, or his emphasis, or the way he went about achieving a result, but it was with the knowledge that Walt's way was always a very good way. Usually each of us felt, "Why didn't I think of that?" But every so often, we secretly would feel, "My way is better" and occasionally it would suddenly seem so to Walt, too. He relied heavily on his staff to feed creative ideas into the mix.

That's not to say he was an easy-going supervisor. When asked "What was Walt like to work with?", his daughter Diane replied:

> Walt was unquestionably one of the most demanding bosses an employee could ever have. He didn't hesitate to cut down

an employee with a harsh word, or even a public tirade. He was uncompromising in his desire for quality, and he held his staff to the same high standards as he held for himself. What's more, he never thought money was the reason to do good work, and he had difficulty understanding others whose main motivation was cash.

And though more than one staffer left the Disney Studio unhappily, many others stayed with Walt for years—some for up to 5 or 6 decades. Thirty years after his death, a number of former employees still welled up with tears when they talked about his passing. This is hardly the mark of a "mean" boss.

Donnie Dunagan, the voice of Bambi, had his own opinion of Walt. He knew what it was like to work with "monsters." At Universal Studios, Dunagan was menaced by Boris Karloff as Frankenstein's Monster in 1939's *Son of Frankenstein* and done in by Karloff as Mord the Executioner in 1939's *Tower of London*. Walt made an indelible impression on young Dunagan as a child, who recalled:

> Mr. Disney was not a pompous executive aristocratic leader. He had his sleeves rolled up. He participated in everything. And when he would come around to an art activity or to a sound activity, People were eager to see him. The employees were eager to see him. The artists were eager to see him. In other studios, when the boss was coming around. People would go, oh gosh, here comes the boss, watch out...watch out. Hide that. Don't ask him. Be quiet. Not with Mr. Disney. Everybody wanted him around because he participated. And he had great ideas, and they would listen to him, in a respectful way, and not like the boss.

This is not to say Walt couldn't be difficult. He was a "bear" from time-to-time. Or, as a reference to a key moment in *Bambi*, whenever Walt was heard coughing as he walked down the hallway, animators would exclaim, "Man is in the forest." Wilfred Jackson, in *Disney Animation, The Illusion of Life*, was quoted as saying,

Some of them felt he was a little rough with them at times. Walt could make you feel real bad when he wanted to. I don't remember them rebelling when he told them to do it different or asked for better animation…Walt was a very persuasive individual and a very inspiring person, and he had the ability to make you want to do what he wanted you to do.

Walt's role was one of creating and sharing ideas, while inspiring others to get on board do the same.

Legacy as Leaders

In short, one studio head manipulated his employees and treated them as commodities. The other treated his employees as vital assets to be given a vision and possibilities.

Both Walt Disney and Louis B. Mayer were demanding bosses. They held high expectations of their employees and were very direct in their approach. Both created unforgettable cinematic experiences. But only one left a legacy with his employees. In the end, that made all the difference in the world. MGM has been bought, sold, and put into bankruptcy several times over. It has been largely dismantled to the point that it is unrecognizable from its glory days.

Meanwhile, the Walt Disney Company has risen to be perhaps the biggest film studio in the world—and the only one whose parent company is still in the greater Los Angeles area. Walt's vision, his approach with his employees, and his leadership have taken the organization to new heights. It's appropriate then, that the studio park experiences in both WDW and in Disneyland Paris are now not named after MGM, but simply Disney himself.

Ideas for the Next Century

Consider how you can make the magic come alive for you:

- What kind of legacy—how people remember you—do you want to leave after it's all over?

- If observed at work, how would a child summarize your behavior?

- How can you expect the best in others, without being unreasonable or overly demanding?

12

Built and Based in Burbank

Creating a Workplace for Employees to Succeed

The success of *Snow White and the Seven Dwarfs* put money in the bank like never before. Instead of keeping it for himself, Walt turned around and invested in a new studio that would be built on the corner of Alameda Avenue and Buena Vista Street in Burbank, California. It would be a new home. But this one would be designed from the ground up.

A World-Class Studio Facility

The new studio would be bigger than the previous Hyperion Studio. But it would be more than just adding size and space. Frank Crowhurst, a structural engineer, and architect assigned to the project recalled "I would sit and listen to animators and story men and different heads of departments—Dave Hand, Ham Luske, Perce Pearce, [Norm] Ferguson—[with] Walt being the voice most of the time. But the things arrived at there were things we did, and it has been shown that they were very practical."

Those practical ideas came in any number of ways, all leading to a facility that modeled in many ways the production pipeline:

- *The Animation Building.* Beginning with Walt's corner office on the top level, the building was designed to model the animation process from storyboards on the top floor, down to completed sequences on the bottom floor. All offices in the 8 corridors of the wings had windows allowing as much natural light as possible. In Art Moderne style, acclaimed designer Kem Weber created special desks and furniture for the animators.

- *The Inking & Painting Building.* Four corridors were built around garden courts to ensure optimum natural light. Its design was large enough to accommodate four hundred desks and a state-of-the art Paint Laboratory. All with one of the first air-conditioning systems on the West Coast, thus controlling humidity. An underground corridor led to the Inking and Painting building from the Animation Building, thus preventing outdoor elements from impacting any art or cel work. A corridor between Ink and Paint and Camera & Cutting also reduced any possibility of this.

- *The Camera & Cutting Building.* Here, all personnel entering the camera rooms passed through a special de-dusting chamber in which twenty separate nozzles blasted air at high velocity to remove lint and dust. The first half included two large multiplane cameras. Editing bays were the focus of the other half. From here the product would come out completed.

- *Vaults.* This group of buildings was for film storage. Since film was made of nitrate, the celluloid was very combustible. These units were constructed so that, in the event of an explosion, the force of it would move upwards blowing off the ceilings.

At the same time the animated process was going on, live-action shooting and audio recording was happening in another section of the property:

- *Stage One.* This large soundstage was the only one built initially, but was soon used for activities such as filming the orchestra during the Leopold Stokowski segments of *Fantasia*, and then during World War II, repairing armed forces trucks and antiaircraft equipment (soundstages have no windows and could therefore be utilized during blackouts).

- *Orchestra Recording, Dialogue Recording,* and *Sound Effects Recording Stages.* Known respectively as Stages A, B, and C, these were three separate buildings to house these activities, and suggests how serious the organization was in providing the best tools and facilities possible. Much of this equipment was still in use when Michael Eisner came in during the 1980s.

- *Theatre Building.* Directly across from the main entrance to The Animation Building, this is where work could be screened.

Other buildings complimented the studio plant to include offices, maintenance, central heating, and, of course, a water tower. In time other soundstages were added as well as backlot buildings, which necessary for television production.

A Park-Like Setting

All these were located in a parklike campus, in the same way one might find nearby universities well landscaped and manicured. A college campus would be a departure from other film studios at the time which seemed in Walt's words to be more like "industrial plants." He noted: "When this place is all finished and landscaped, it will have a very magnificent feeling about it. You go over to any motion picture lot, and you will find a street twenty feet wide so trucks can get about and buildings fifty or sixty feet high. They are long alleyways." Streets were given names like Minnie Avenue and Dopey Drive.

Even color tones were thought out. Frank Crowhurst noted "We thought at that time we should get some sense of California colors or desert colors or something that would be gay rather than the somberness of dark red brick. This resulted in a palette of green, red, and beige earth tones that were eventually carried over to the Disney-MGM Studios when it opened. It's a look that is still signature to the studio today.

An "Employee-Friendly" Place

But beyond the landscaping, Walt intended a different sort of culture. Others before him had created factory towns, but he really visualized something that would "feel" different. Long before Google made places that were "googly" and other companies would build similar "employee friendly" environments, Walt included the following:

- Horseshoe courts & Ping Pong tables
- Volleyball court & a Baseball field
- Fields for picnic events
- The Commissary, known as the Walt Disney Studio Restaurant
- First floor coffee shop in the Animation Building
- A tearoom lounge in the Ink and Painting Building with accompanying patios known as the Inkwell and the Paintwell
- Food delivered to your office
- Dry cleaning available
- A Penthouse Club featuring a full gymnasium, dining rooms, a sun deck, a barbershop, and massage room

Organizations today like Google, Genentech, and Apple implement these kinds of amenities into their employee's experience. In many ways, Disney was a pioneer in creating a place where employees could work in a supportive physical environment that would meet their needs. But we will also see that one of those amenities would become a thorn in the side of Walt's effort to build a great place to work.

At the same time, they were building a new "home" for their artists, Roy and Walt were providing a new home for their parents as part of a 50th Anniversary present to their parents. It came with a "good heating system"—or so they thought. But soon it malfunctioned. The brothers had a couple of studio workers come out to repair it. On the morning of November 26th, 1938, carbon monoxide poisoning from the defective heater spread through the house. Their housekeeper and a neighbor dragged both Flora and Elias out of the house. Elias would recover. Flora did not. Both brothers were devastated—Walt especially. Years later, when his daughter Sharon asked about it, Walt snapped, "I don't want to talk about it." When in South America a few years later Elias passed away while he was out of the country.

Ideas for the Next Century

Consider how you can make the magic come alive for you:

- How do you invest in making it easier for others to do their work?

- How does your physical environment support your ability to get the job done?

- How does your physical environment support the quality and productivity of the work performed?

- What messages does your work environment say about your culture?

13

Strike!

The Sting When Others Oppose You

When Employee Expectations Aren't Yours

It would seem that a new studio facility designed perfectly for its artists would make everyone happy, especially compared to the makeshift facilities that were at the Hyperion Studio before it. It was one way for Walt to reward his employees while building an organization that could produce more animated fare in the years to come. But several factors came together as the studio moved into its new Burbank facility:

1. A celebratory event for *Snow White and the Seven Dwarfs* was held one weekend at the luxurious Lake Norconian Club. Artists expected that Walt would announce big bonuses for this event, similar to how they were offered when creating the shorts. Walt made a big presentation that evening, talking about the future, but never mentioning bonuses, which left everyone confused. That led to artists becoming raucous for the rest of their stay. Walt left the event early frustrated when he saw the poor behavior of this staff.

2. Bonuses did come later that summer, but they were a fraction of what many had received from the release of earlier shorts—even though record box office numbers were made with *Snow White*. Disney animators had the best working conditions one could ask for in the industry. But they also worked long hours and faced

very difficult deadlines. The pay structure was varied and somewhat disorganized, and some didn't even get a bonus.

3. The 1930s and its accompanying Great Depression resulted in a large number of labor unions being created. This included the Screen Cartoonist's Guild, which by this time had organized every animation studio but one—Disney.

4. With European markets being closed off due to an impending war, and with rising costs in creating new animated product, beautifully created products like *Pinocchio* and *Fantasia* failed to do well in the box office. Soon thereafter layoffs were involved.

5. Iconic to the new studio was Walt's thought of rewarding his top animators with access to the Penthouse suite. At Hyperion, the organization seemed flatter—just like "family." Now it seemed as though there were favorites and a hierarchy. As animator Ken Peterson described: "When we moved to the new studio, Walt's paternalism was expressed in the Penthouse Club. The dividing line for membership was money; you had to earn two hundred a week, something like that. I didn't qualify and a lot of others didn't either."

All of this occurred during a time when *Pinocchio* and *Fantasia* were released and as *Dumbo* and *Bambi* were in production. Discussions and meetings were held with key animators and others as they sought to organize a union. This was personally hurtful for Walt, who had worked tirelessly for almost 20 years to create a great studio as well as a positive place to work. It led Walt to experience one of the most painful episodes of his career. When a strike finally launched, Walt took it personally, and perhaps understandably so. After all, so much of the profits were applied toward creating a better space for everyone to enjoy. He probably didn't see the effect that one little "club" could have on the entire culture, or that the pay seemed erratic much less unfair. Even Walt himself, while having an office suite, had a working arrangement that was very modest compared to the Hollywood moguls of that time.

In February of 1941, he gathered all of the employees together and laid his concerns, frustrations, and pain on the table. He told of he and his brother's own sacrifices in meeting payroll over the years and that some half a million had been distributed in bonuses and adjustments. He talked about present concerns, the escalating war, and the challenges in meeting payroll. Then he stated at the end that it was still the right of employees to organize and join any labor organization of their choosing, and the Company did not have a right to interfere.

A Well-Drawn Picket Line

By the end of May 1941, a picket line was formed in front of the Studio. About 40% were striking and the other 60% remained on the job. It didn't help that the artists created some of the most visually interesting picket signs, which made it easier for the *Los Angeles Times* and other press outlets to put the strike in their headlines. Also, ironic that *The Reluctant Dragon* was in theaters around the same time as the strike was going on. After all, a large part of the film leading up to *The Reluctant Dragon* short itself was showcasing Disney's new Burbank studio and how fantastic it was to work there.

Emotionally, Walt was all over the place. As described in Bob Thomas's biography of Walt, on the second day of the strike, he stood inside the studio gate and yelled back "Aw, they'll be back in a couple of days." In another instance as he drove his car across picket lines and into his parking space, he overheard one animator over a loudspeaker: "There he is—the man who believes in brotherhood for everybody but himself." Walt threw off his coat and headed toward the man when studio police blocked him from making a more regrettable choice.

There were many sympathetic to Walt during this time: In Mindy Johnson's *Ink & Paint*, Grace Godino stated "It wasn't for the money…I felt I was wrong to do this. I had been treated so well at [Disney] that I saw no point. Why should I kick a person in the face that gave me this opportunity that I was so happy with and that I enjoyed, and I was learning?"

Jean Erwin also from *Ink & Paint* observed: "It was a very emotional strike. Extremely emotional[,] and Walt was emotional about it[,] and he should have been. The older I get, I can see his view more. He wanted to put money back into the business. He was very farsighted, but we were very shortsighted."

A "Family" Divided

In the end, Walt commented :

> To me, the entire situation is a catastrophe. The spirit that played such an important part in the building of the cartoon medium has been destroyed…I was willing to sacrifice everything I had and would have fought to the last ditch had it not been for the fact that a lot of innocent people might have been hurt….I am thoroughly disgusted and would gladly quit and try to establish myself in another business if it were not for the loyal guys who believe in me—so I guess I'm stuck with it.

Animator Marc Davis summed it up this way:

> I think the strike changed everybody…I think that Walt became resigned that he had to operate in a more hard-nosed way, like a lot of other people who have something forced on them that they don't like. I don't say that he was less benevolent. But I think that a lot of the frills that he thought were so wonderful when we first came out to the new building…went by the boards. I'm sure that he had to feel that [the strike] was a thing against him personally, and I guess in some areas it certainly was.

The desire Walt had to build a world-class studio for his employees, something where people would feel at home, was at the heart of his decision in building a fantastic studio complex. And yet, he felt terribly misunderstood. He couldn't understand why many of his key artists felt so differently about his treatment toward them.

Ideas for the Next Century

Consider how you can make the magic come alive for you:

- How well are you listening to others around you and their needs?

- Do others buy in to what you have to offer and what you are trying to do for them?

- Can you honestly say that you care more of others than any other organization or entity?

14

Uniting with South America

Working to Connect Others

Walt was left devastated by the strike. He saw himself as a very giving employer, who took care of his employee's needs. How could his artists turn against him and go on strike when everyone needed to come together?

A World Divided

Division at the studio, painful as it was, was not nearly what was happening globally. As if the strike early in 1941 was not enough, events leading to a second world war were unfolding and impacting everyone—even the tiny Disney Studios in Burbank California. European markets were collapsing; and they were a source of profit for Disney films like *Bambi* and *Fantasia*.

Nazi and Fascist influence of Germany and Italy had stretched well across the European continent making the United States government concerned about its influence on South America. The last thing the United States needed was for all or part of South America to take sides with the Third Reich.

Even at home things were happening. There were conflicts and ethnic prejudice against Mexico, especially along the border. As J.B. Kaufman's *South of the Border with Disney* articulated: "South America was distant enough from the U.S. that it could easily be portrayed in the mass media in exotic, glamorous terms. Mexico...was a different story. An uneasy racial tension, fueled by direct contact, had been brewing in the most heavily populated U.S. cities for several decades, and it found a particularly ugly outlet in the wartime atmosphere of the early 1940s. The infamous "Zoot Suit Riots," capping more than a year of escalating hostilities, erupted in the streets of Los Angeles as gangs of U.S. servicemen openly attacked Mexican neighborhoods."

A Good Will Tour

Nelson Rockefeller, Coordinator of Inter-American Affairs (CIAA), had been tasked by President Roosevelt to identify ways of developing a closer relationship with Latin American countries. Conversations started with Roy and then included Walt. The idea initially was to encourage the studios in doing some shorts that had a Latin American feel to them. The studios had already dubbed and distributed films like *Snow White* and *Pinocchio* in Spanish and Portuguese—at great cost. But this would be something more, something different. As correspondence continued, they approached Walt about doing a goodwill tour.

Walt resisted the idea, as he simply couldn't envision himself on some ambassadorial tour. Rockefeller countered by suggesting Walt go create a movie down there. The government also offered to cover travel expenses and provide financial support for the pictures they produced.

Returning to Kaufman: "Clearly the cause of hemispheric unity had a long way to go. The efforts of Walt and his staff on behalf of the Good Neighbor program, exercising care to create a motion picture that might truly help to cement relations between the U.S. and Mexico, take on added significance against this backdrop."

The offer from Nelson Rockefeller was enough for Roy Disney to encourage Walt to get away from the studio and allow Roy time and space to heal the wounds left open by the strike.

Soon a team of seventeen amigos (pals), known as *"Walt y el Grupo"* ("Walt and the Group") left in August of that same year for a twelve-week trip. Over the duration of this trip and others, the team would see countries like Argentina, Bolivia, Brazil, Chile, Colombia, Bolivia, Mexico. Panama, and Peru.

Amigos and Caballeros—Always Together

The result of the trip and others resulted in two major feature films: *Saludos Amigos*, and *The Three Caballeros*. *Saludos Amigos* shows the "*Walt y el Grupo*" in South America among shorts focused on a plane named Pedro navigating Argentina and Chile by way of Aconcagua. Goofy is then featured as a gaucho in Argentina. It culminates with Jose Carioca and Donald meeting up in Brazil.

In *The Three Caballeros* Donald receives presents that turn into stories focusing on a South Pole penguin heading to warmer waters. Then it turns to a flying gauchito and burro in the Pampas of Argentina. Finally, it picks up with Jose Carioca joining Donald in Mexico as they meet up with Panchito—forming *The Three Caballeros*.

Both films are a collection of shorts, but their combination was at the suggestion of David O. Selznick who suggested that a combined format would give greater credibility to the government's efforts to encourage unity.

There were also other individual celluloid products that came out of this experience. Entertainment shorts like *Pluto and the Armadillo*, which included Mickey and his dog visiting Brazil, in 1943 as well as *Pelican and the Snipe* in 1944 were such examples. *Blame It on the Samba* starring Donald Duck and Jose Carioca would join a connected series of shorts released as *Melody Time* in 1948.

Moreover, the CIAA asked Disney to create a series of literacy and health-related shorts for Latin America. Such was *The Winged Scourge* of 1943, where Dopey and the rest of the dwarfs seek to eradicate malaria. One educational film made in 1944 was called *The Amazon Awakens*, and was largely a live action documentary, combined with moments of animation. It would be a predecessor for *True-Life Adventures* as well as the *People & Places* series Disney would create a few years later.

74

According to the CIAA, these films were well received. "I am happy to be able to report that both the health films and the literacy films have been successful far beyond our expectations."

Though these times were difficult, the cumulative work of Walt and the studio did have a positive effect, not only on North and South American relations, but on helping the Walt Disney Productions Studio recover from a bitter strike. It also supported the studio fiscally during a difficult financial time.

At the end of this collaboration with the CIAA Kaufman observes :

> But by now the experience of his [Walt's] Latin American years had been absorbed into the fabric of his studio. The Disney artists had responded to the challenges of the Good Neighbor project with fresh new ideas and techniques, and now the studio continued to build on those innovative animation concepts…and so they live on today, remarkable souvenirs of a unique chapter in Disney history—colorful, exhilarating films that once strove to unite a hemisphere.

The message of these films can be found in the lyrics of *The Three Caballeros*. It is as timely as ever:

> *We're happy amigos,*
>
> *No matter where he goes,*
>
> *The one, two and three goes.*
>
> *We're always together.*

Ideas for the Next Century

Consider how you can make the magic come alive for you:

- How can serving and connecting with others give greater context and focus to your own personal challenges and circumstances?

- What greater good can draw you together with those around you as you seek to help others?

- What can you learn from others about being a more cohesive organization?

15

The New Spirit

Do You Have a Mickey Mouse Operation?

That's what the IRS told Walt Disney in the 1940s. Curiously, it's
not a pejorative remark. In fact, it was really a compliment. You
need some context to understand what was happening.

Donald Duck to the Rescue

The country was embroiled in a war to end all wars, and everybody
had to contribute. Americans helped the war effort through victory
gardens, collecting scrap paper, iron, and rubber drives, and with
woman working in the factories to keep manufacturing going.

The impact was even more profound at the Disney studios. Already
international markets were being cut off, and many of Walt's artists
were leaving to fight overseas. But then came the attack on Pearl
Harbor on December 7, 1941. The U.S. Army had taken over the
studio to fix tanks in the soundstages during California blackouts.
(Soundstages have no windows.) Even Walt had to have
identification to get onto his own studio lot.

By 6 pm the following evening, the Navy's Bureau of Supplies and
Accounts had made a contract with Walt Disney to produce twenty
training films on aircraft and warship identification. This became
known as WEFT (Wings, Engine, Fuselage, Tail) series, and the
Navy became one of the studio's largest clients. Soon the Army
signal corps, the Army Air Force, and the Air Transport Command

signed contracts with the Disney Studio. Within a few years, Disney produced nearly one hundred training films. They also produced a number of propaganda shorts targeted at the enemy, such as *Education for Death*, and *Der Fuehrer's Face*, which won an Academy Award for best short subject (Cartoon). So much of the work at this time was focused on the war effort.

Around this same time, U.S. Secretary of the Treasury Henry Morgenthau sought out Walt Disney to make a picture about the patriotic duty of paying income tax, something that many, if not most, Americans were still not doing. Disney had just made four Canadian shorts to help sell savings bonds. Those included Mickey and the gang, the Three Little Pigs, and even the Seven Dwarfs. At a reasonable price, Walt offered his leading man, Donald Duck, to make the pitch. The resulting short, *The New Spirit*, was shown everywhere, and created a higher level of compliance. Morgenthau did not see Donald as a good choice. He envisioned a "Mr. Average Taxpayer." Walt Disney countered this, noting that loaning out Donald Duck for an incentive film was equal to MGM loaning out a Clark Gable. After all, at that time, Donald Duck was the studio's biggest star.

Walt Disney won the debate. Donald became "Mr. Average Taxpayer." Production on the film did not start until December 18th. Since the purpose of the film was to convince people to pay their taxes by April 15th of the following spring, production on the film proceeded at a staggering pace. Other than the impressions of Morgenthau and Disney, little research concerning the use of Donald Duck went into the film. However, studies did confirm the film's effectiveness. A Gallup Poll reported that some 37 percent of those who had seen the film felt it had affected their willingness to pay taxes. This is significant, considering the Treasury Department reported that *The New Spirit* was seen by 32,647,000 people in 11,800 theaters.

One Good Deed Deserves an Audit

But in a classic act of bureaucracy, Congress scoffed at paying for a cartoon in the middle of a war, and Walt's organization was audited.

When the auditors took a look at Disney's books, they found nothing inappropriate, but they did exclaim, "This sure is a Mickey Mouse operation!"

Walt took the comment as a compliment, as it was...sort of. Mickey Mouse is a simple character made of basic circles and lines. The expression meant you have a very simple, easy approach to doing your accounting books.

So, ask yourself, when it comes to how you do business, would you like to be called a "Mickey Mouse Operation"? Or for that matter, would you like to be called an "Apple Operation"? A "Tesla Operation"? Or a "JetBlue Operation"? Any of those terms might express the thought that your organization was cool, radical, or fun, respectively. What these and other great organizations have in common is that they are focused on their customers.

Ideas for the Next Century

Consider how you can make the magic come alive for you:

- Do you have a Mickey Mouse operation?

- How simple and streamlined is your operation?

- How would you describe your operation or the work you do?

- What would it take for other organizations to want to imitate what you do best?

16

Victory Through Air Power

Doing Something for the Greater Good

While there were efforts like *Saludos Amigos* and *The Three Caballeros* during this time, the studio nearly halted all feature-length animated films of the caliber Disney had defined with *Snow White* through *Bambi* during the war. The most obscure of these, and one no longer listed on Disney's official list of such films, is *Victory Through Air Power*.

A Film Offering an End to the War

This film was based on a book of the same title written by Major Alexander de Seversky. During the thirties, de Seversky had accomplished several feats in the field of aviation. The film outlined how the strategic use of long-range bombing could conquer both Japan and Germany, and thus end the war. Walt Disney was so impressed with the book that he purchased the screen rights to the film and hired de Seversky as a technical advisor and key player. It would not be a family film. This would be Walt's effort to advocate a path for ending a terrible war.

This was new and risky territory, choosing to finance a film out of pocket to promote the war effort. Unlike the CIAA films in Latin America, or the Treasury and other government-funded training and propaganda films, this was on Walt's own dollar. Early on the critical question that came up was who would want to see this film. By now Walt Disney had sized up his audience when it came to *Dumbo* and

Bambi. But here Disney was not only concerned about the audience response, but about the timelessness of the film itself.

Would Anyone See This Film?

The Audience Research Institute was paid $5,000 to conduct a Gallup Poll on audience reaction and publicity penetration on a Reader's Digest version of de Seversky's writings, previously released. The survey reported that a month after the release of the Reader's Digest version, 20 million people had heard of de Seversky and that five million had read either the Reader's Digest version or the actual book. It also showed that 78 percent would want to see the film.

But there were two bigger concerns. First, the name Walt Disney is known for humor and *Victory* was a serious departure from that. Second, people tend to exaggerate "their intention of doing what they feel they ought to do," meaning intent to see the film didn't mean they would actually show up. The conclusion was that this type of project was probably not the kind of activity for which the Disney name was best suited, and that such a project carried some risk to Disney's reputation.

Despite all of this, Walt took the gamble and moved forward to make the film. Notes from the story conferences reflect concern that the film be simply told in order to appeal to a general audience, yet not be so simplistic as to discount the material for lack of details. During one production meeting, Walt was concerned with the plausibility of some of the guns, bombsights, and planes used, many of which were still in formative stages of design. He commented: "We've got to be careful that everything we do here is plausible. We've got to build it up so that the people are convinced that they are right with us on this. If we get too fantastic, it is going to cause people to discount the whole thing."

The film premiered on July 17, 1943, to mixed reactions. Particularly skeptical were the Navy and Army which, according to de Seversky's ideas, would take a back seat to air power. The film violated Walt Disney's cardinal rule of timelessness. It was soon outdated and never returned to the theater. It did break even, however, earning revenues just above the cost of production.

Film critic James Agee criticized the political philosophies of the film, but in doing so, gave a backhanded compliment to how the film was presented: "I only hope Major de Seversky and Walt Disney know what they are talking about, for I suspect an awful lot of people who see *Victory Through Air Power* are going to think they do."

The Disney Difference at Normandy

Curiously, the importance of the film and its message was not played out in movie theaters, but rather behind closed doors. One pivotal player in the war, Winston Churchill, was impressed with the film, and in August of 1943, asked President Franklin D. Roosevelt if he had ever seen the film. When Roosevelt replied that he had not, a print was rushed to Quebec where a conference was being held to discuss plans for the forthcoming Allied invasions of Italy and France. Together they watched it twice. According to an insider, Roosevelt was "much excited about the way Disney's aircraft masterfully wiped ships off the seas. It was run again the next day, and then FDR invited the Joint Chiefs to have a look at it. This played an important role in the decision, which was then taken, to give the D-Day invasion sufficient air power. The film had an unexpected influence on D-Day, June 6, 1944.

Again, in Walt's mind it was not about the box office. It was about ending the war. And in the years since, it has been removed from Disney's vaults. It was a unique film for a unique time. But it may have made more of a difference than people will ever know.

Ideas for the Next Century

Consider how you can make the magic come alive for you:

- What beliefs and values do you hold that could have greater implications far beyond you and the work you do?

- How do you measure the potential success of risks you may undertake?

- Which of your beliefs are you willing to take risks for without any guarantee of success or payoff?

- Are there ways you make a difference people may never know?

17

Fun and Fancy Free

Acting When the Choices Are Limited

Fun and Fancy Free was the name of an anthology or package film created by Walt and his studio team. It was the fourth of six such package films produced in the 1940s. Referenced earlier was *Saludos Amigos* and *The Three Caballeros*. But *Make Mine Music, Melody Time,* and *Adventures of Icabod and Mr. Toad* were also such package films. *Fun and Fancy Free* starts off with Jiminy Cricket, then moves into a story of Bongo, a circus bear who falls in love. Later the film showcases Mickey, Donald, and Goofy in a parody of Jack and the Beanstalk.

Anything But Fun and Fancy Free

The statement "fun and fancy free" also refers to the idea of having the freedom to find your own delight. This would not be the situation for Walt at this time. After the world toppled two global giants in World War II, the company had more than $4 million in debts, and business was very slow in the war's aftermath. The company began again distributing films in Europe, but they had difficulty getting monies to come back to the Studios in the United States. It was difficult to return to the kind of focus and effort generated by the studio in the first films starting with *Snow White*. While these were feature-length features, the actual length was often shorter, and the films filled more of a B-film role for a double feature rather than as a headliner. There are many moments of terrific

animation throughout these films. But they are just that—
moments—and it's difficult to acknowledge any of these films in the
same category of the studio's earlier classic-style work. Looking back,
it's amazing that Walt and Roy kept the lights on. But the work itself
still fell short of what he knew he was capable of.

As Walt remarked: "We're through with caviar. From now on its
mashed potato and gravy." The post-war menu looked bleak to Roy
Disney as well when it became impossible, in the postwar depression,
to get payments from abroad—as monies were blocked from leaving
the countries. How did they make it through these times? There
were two ways in which they led during this time:

Lean on Your Prior Reputation

At one point, the Los Angeles liaison for Bank of America wanted
Walt and Roy to discuss their business affairs up in San Francisco.
The studios debts were up, and the revenues were low. When they
arrived for the meeting, there were twelve directors all sitting around
the table. Moreover, A. P. Giannini, the founder and board
chairman of Bank of America was present. A. P. listened to the
discussion around the table. The brothers struggled to offer hope in
light of the war and the closed markets.

In Bob Thomas's work on Walt, he noted that "Giannini began
interrogating the directors: 'I've been lending the Disneys lots of
money—how many of their pictures have you seen? Which ones? He
demanded answers from each board member, and he discovered
that several of them had seen none of the Disney movies. Then
Giannini pointed out:

> Well, I've seen them…I've been watching the Disneys'
> pictures quite closely, because I knew we were lending them
> money far above the financial risk. But I realized that there's
> nothing about those pictures that will be changed by the war.
> They're good this year, they're good next year, and they're
> good the year after. Now there's a war on and the Disneys'
> markets are in trouble. Their money's frozen or else they

can't get in countries. You have to relax and give them time to market their product. This war isn't going to last forever.

With that Giannini strode out of the room. Walt and Roy returned to Los Angeles with the assurance that they would be able to stay in business.

The brothers got through these difficult moments because they kept a long-term vision and associated with individuals who held the same. They earned the trust of Bank of America's founder and board chairman because of the hard work they had done. That would pay dividends in their favor for decades to come.

It's Whatcha Do with Whatcha Got

Despite assurances from Giannini himself, finances tied Walt's hands tightly. Inside of him was a creative soul who had to focus more on "making do with what you got" than with "making the sky the limit." In fact, "It's What You Do with Whatcha Got" is a song found in a film he made at that time, entitled *So Dear to My Heart*. One of the things that Walt took advantage of during this time was the fact that he had a full, complete studio. With soundstages and recording studios, he could reach beyond just doing animation, which was painfully slow and very expensive to create.

For example, one of his first attempts was a feature that offered a tour of his new studio. Mentioned earlier, *The Reluctant Dragon* showed American Humorist Robert Benchley walking all over the new studio to try to find Walt to pitch an idea for a short. While it came out during the difficult and embarrassing episode of the strike, it was his first foray into live action. Live action allowed the studio to create a product much quicker than the arduous process of animation. Walt Disney Productions needed to embrace live-action production that used their studios, their assets, and most importantly, their reputation. It would be characterized as family entertainment, with some films infused with bits and pieces of animation.

So, Walt turned his focus on live-action projects. An anonymous animator stated in Bob Thomas's book on Walt Disney: "As soon as Walt rode on a camera crane…we knew we were going to lose him."

The sense of control Walt Disney had in producing a live-action film was a contrast to the many animated film projects that kept escalating in cost. Many of these animation projects never saw the light of day. Others, like *Alice in Wonderland* dragged on for years—even during the era of *Snow White*—and took years to complete. In the instance of *Destino*, a project made in collaboration with Salvador Dali, the project was shelved for decades until 2003 when, with the support of Walt's nephew, Roy E. Disney, it was completed.

Roy O. Disney's biography would remark: "We are not going into these things because we are feeling our oats or getting ambitious…We are doing it for common-sense business reasons, realizing the hazards of our basic cartoon business."

Song of the South in 1946 and *So Dear to My Heart* in 1948 allowed Walt to use live action to counter the costs of animation that would be interspersed in each of those films. These efforts along with the films being created in Europe brought the Disney organization into a new business era.

In time, Walt Disney Studios became known as well for its movies as it did for its animation. In time films like *Mary Poppins*, *Swiss Family Robinson*, *Pollyanna*, and *The Parent Trap* owe their success to the fact that Walt had to make do with what he had and extend his business into film production.

Ideas for the Next Century

Consider how you can make the magic come alive for you:

- What are the "meat and potatoes" of your business? Can you make those ingredients come alive?

- Have there been times when life was not "Fun and Fancy Free"? What is it about those periods that is most frustrating?

- How do you "Do with Whatcha Got" when faced with those circumstances?

18

True Life Adventures

Controlling Fate at Home and Abroad

One opportunity and one need merged at the same time. When they came together, they created a greater opportunity for Disney.

RKO

In the early years, Disney created a film but getting it into the theaters was a different matter. In the first decade that answer came in the form of United Artists (UA), who distributed shorts for the company. But United Artists had a different opinion on *Snow White and the Seven Dwarfs*. They felt that it needed to be a romance. Walt saw it differently and the result was an end to their distribution with UA.

Disney signed up with **RKO** Pictures, one of the "Big Five" film studios during that golden era of film making. Films like *It's a Wonderful Life* and *Citizen Cane,* and actors the likes of Katharine Hepburn and Cary Grant were the results of this very successful production and distribution firm. Association such as this was not only helpful in getting its first full-length feature, *Snow White and the Seven Dwarfs,* out into full distribution—it was an approach very much needed and also very different than simply getting short films out into the theaters.

This arrangement continued on for a full two decades. In the process, the eccentric tycoon Howard Hughes sought to take over the company. In Bob Thomas's book about Roy Disney, the first meeting with Howard Hughes and Roy Disney began at an office bungalow attached to the Beverly Hills Hotel. His assistant directed Roy to meet up with Hughes in the men's room. Roy found him standing next to a urinal, and Roy joined in at the next stall before moving back over to the office. It was peculiar at best. But it continued on with calls in the middle of the night, a practice of Hughes since he often began his workday at midnight. In receiving such a call, Edna answered fearing some family catastrophe. It was Hughes asking to speak with Roy. "No, you may not. My husband works hard all day, and he deserves his rest. If you want to speak to him, call him during the regular business hours. Good night, Mr. Hughes." Even Edna Disney was not going to let Howard Hughes control her sleep.

Hughes eccentricities were one thing. His ability to run RKO was another. Actor Dick Powell was believed to have said, "RKO's contract list is down to three actors and 127 lawyers." It came to a head at Disney when RKO became reluctant to release the *True-Life Adventures* series.

True-Life Adventures

The concept behind *True-Life Adventure* films first came around with *The Amazon Awakens*. This film was one of the first good-neighbor pictures produced for the CIAA during World War II. The picture is primarily Amazon Basin footage taken by a husband-and-wife photography team. Ben Sharpsteen, an artist for the company, noted that anthropomorphism—building plot by giving a real animal various human characteristics—was first used by Walt Disney in this film. For many years, Walt Disney admired the work of Pare Lorentz, a documentary film maker of the thirties, and perhaps sought to contribute something notable to the field himself.

As Congress worked to pass legislation to make Alaska and Hawaii the 49th and 50th states of the Union, there was genuine interest across the country for not just these two territories, but for exploring the world beyond the continental United States. Passenger aviation was a new thing that enabled people to go beyond where their car took them.

Walt could see the curiosity toward other lands, people, and places. He reached out to a wildlife magazine editor. That individual told Walt to check out a short wildlife film by Alfred and Elma Milotte. In 1948, Walt reached out to them and invited them to work for the studio to shoot film on location in Alaska. Walt and his daughter Sharon even headed to Alaska to visit the couple as they worked.

Alfred later recalled, "Walt was great. He said, 'Just go out and get some good pictures.' He never told us how to do it. He gave us independence." That freedom allowed Al and Elma to get the footage they needed. It also made Walt think more deeply about how he could set things in motion, giving people the freedom and tools along with the vision, then pull back and play more of an executive producer role.

The labor for doing these films was small. It often constituted a couple willing to go out into the wild. That wild would consist of extreme climate and environmental challenges. It involved going where no roads were and encountering nature sometimes at its worst moment. Moreover, the challenge was taking cameras, equipment, and plenty of film. The ratio of film shot to film used in the final cut was huge compared to a standard studio film which would be scripted, directed, and then shot. *Seal Island* shot more than 100,000 feet of film. The total production cost Disney a little over $100,000.

An Opportunity and Need Merges

Walt's team back home would take the endless reels of film and navigate through it until they found something of substance that they could make a story out of—herds of seals on a particular Alaskan island. The people who couldn't get their head around it was RKO—responsible for distributing the film. In an era where double features were common, RKO expected full-length or short film length selections. But the *True-Life Adventures* films were only as long as they were interesting. And that length often placed them between a short and full-length.

Walt convinced a theatrical owner in Pasadena to show the film on a one-run distribution in December of 1948. This favor qualified the film to be nominated for an Academy Award. *Seal Island* won that award for best documentary. Walt took the trophy down to Roy the next morning and told him to take it and bang the heads of the executives at RKO with it.

By the time *The Living Desert* premiered in 1953, Roy Disney established his own team of salespeople and methodically began to distribute the film along with the short, *Ben and Me*, to select theaters starting in New York City. Thus, was born Buena Vista Distribution (Buena Vista was a street that bordered the Walt Disney Studios and would eventually become the title of the main boulevard that would serve as the entrance of Disney California Adventure). In time, small Buena Vista offices were opened across the country in major cities with salesman in each working with Roy to get Disney films distributed. Films were released by Buena Vista, which means "good view" in Spanish. That "good view" came when the Disney brothers merged an opportunity with a need.

Ideas for the Next Century

Consider how you can make the magic come alive for you:

- What is the "Good View" or "Buena Vista" for what you do?

- How can you give support and direction yet allow others to act for themselves?

- Where do you need to take control of your fate and fortune?

- Where could opportunity and need merge for you?

19

The Locomotion of a Hobby

How to Reignite the Fire within You

"The Lost Years"

As the 1940s ended, Walt went through a series of starts and stops in an effort to try to figure out how to create a solid offering of full-length animated features. *Cinderella*, *Peter Pan*, *Alice in Wonderland* were all under development, and with the latter, it was difficult to nail down the story.

Roy O. Disney described these as "the lost years." He told Walt after a heated exchange one night: "Look, you're letting this place drive you to the nuthouse. That's one place I'm not going with you!" Still, Walt struggled to deal with the stress he was facing. That night neither Walt nor Roy slept well. The next morning, Roy shared:

> I'm at my desk, wondering what the hell to do. We were in a hell of a fix, tight payroll on our hands and everything. You don't worry about yourself, you worry about your commitments, your involvements.
>
> I felt awfully low. I heard his cough and his footsteps coming down the hall. He came in and he was filled up, he could hardly talk. He says, 'Isn't it amazing what a horse's ass a fellow can be sometimes?' And he walked out. That's how we settled our differences.

Roy also suggested that Walt find a hobby. He took up an interest in trains. There were several experiences and events that led toward this interest.

A "Train" of Ideas

Growing up in the mid-west at the beginning of the 20th century, the train was a major technological achievement. His Uncle Mike was an engineer on the Santa Fe line running between Walt's home in Marceline and Fort Madison, Iowa. In his youth, Walt would be a news butcher on board hawking candy, sodas, fruit, and tobacco out of a wooden box carried at waist level.

Walt came to Los Angeles on the Santa Fe California Limited in 1923. Later, the ideas around a new character who would be named Mickey Mouse came on a train from New York to Los Angeles. Many train rides took him on business and leisure trips across the country. Trains showed up in many of his animated shorts and even films, such as the Casey Jr. Circus Train in *Dumbo*.

So Dear to My Heart, which was a love letter to his childhood in Marceline, begins with a train heading into the Fulton Corners station. Animator Ward Kimball, a big train fan, often advised Walt on details when it came to including trains. He even had his own small-scale train in his backyard. Walt offered the entire Fulton Corners station to Ward after the film. The design of this station would eventually be used for the station in Frontierland at Disneyland.

In the 1939 Golden Gate International Exposition, Walt became enamored with an exhibition of miniature rooms depicting interiors from the 17th century to the 1930s. Walt took on this hobby— building out Granny Kincaid's cabin, complete with a hand-braided rug, an ornate stone fireplace, and a guitar with small strings. At one point, Walt considered doing an entire exhibit that would be carried on a train tour. Walt named the project *Disneylandia*.

Studio nurse, Hazel George, knew about Walt's stress quite well during this period. She recommended that Walt head out to see the

Chicago Railroad Fair, which hosted an exhibit of 100 years of American railroading. Walt invited Ward Kimball to come along with him. Taking the *Super Chief* from Pasadena, they were invited to ride in the engine and pull the cord to blow the whistle. Ward observed that Walt "just sat there staring into space, smiling and smiling…I had never seen him look so happy." They would also go to Dearborn, Michigan, to take in the Henry Ford Museum.

Building Your Own Railroad

Coming back from these events, Walt was not just rejuvenated but spinning with ideas. This coincided with the purchase of a new home on five acres in Los Angeles' Holmby Hills neighborhood on a street named Carolwood Drive. He commenced building a backyard railway named after the street he lived on as the Carolwood Pacific. From an article written in *Railroad Magazine*, Walt had a lawyer write up right-of-way agreements to go under his wife's flowers and landscaping with a tunnel. But Lillian could probably see how freeing it was to see Walt focused on a hobby, and he loved to take guests around his back yard riding on top of these steam trains that were only 1/8 scale. Walt named the engine "Lilly Belle."

Beyond animator Ward Kimball, Walt utilized the talents of Roger Broggie and other machinists who worked at the machine shop at the studio. After work, Walt would step up to the bench with them as he worked on his projects. He found some landscapers in Jack and Bill Evans to help provide park-like landscaping in a way that his wife would favor.

These individuals were among the pioneers that would eventually help make a real-life park come alive. Originally these ideas were combined in a small plot of land adjacent to the studio, given the name of Mickey Mouse Park. Studio production designer Harper Goff created the illustrations. He, too, would be an important player in what would eventually unfold.

Soon thereafter it became obvious that these ideas were bigger than the land could hold. Walt went looking for a much bigger parcel—he found one in a place known as Anaheim. Small wonder when the first drawing was created over a weekend, the instructions were to include a train running around it.

Ideas for the Next Century

Consider how you can make the magic come alive for you:

- Have you experienced lost days, weeks, months, or even years? Where did they go, and why?

- How can a hobby or outside interest help you deal with your daily stress and struggle?

- Who can support your hobbies and interests? Who can help you make your dreams come alive?

20

Cinderella

A Transformation Begins

From Chaos to Order

At the heart of Cinderella is a girl who is more than a scullery maid, but rather an emerging princess. That transformation comes because of a fairy godmother, who gives Cinderella the tools and opportunities to go to the ball. Walt shared that the moment of Cinderella's transformation into a new dress by the Fairy Godmother was his favorite animation of all.

That transformation is at the heart of where Walt may likely have been. With a hobby helping him to see the forest apart from the trees, he begins to emerge not so much as the creator but the producer. Neal Gabler's work on Walt Disney summarizes this best during the time in which *Cinderella* was finishing production:

> Walt supervised, as always, and his was the final word, but he was considerably less involved than on *Snow White* or even *Dumbo*, and some of the staff complained about it. "Walt is not an artist," one former employee told a reporter. "He doesn't have the instincts or the imagination of an artist. His little-known virtue is that of a great producer, who happens to recognize the importance of putting out a product technically better than anyone else's." Another employee described Walt's demeanor as more "businesslike" now, less excitable but also less exciting.

Perhaps to survive, diversify and most importantly to grow, Walt had to leave the creative minutiae and focus on building a successful studio. With show business, there is the show, and there is the business. After the war, neither was successfully occurring. And it was hard to get the cart before the horse.

In Walt and Roy O. Disney's biographies by Bob Thomas, there is this moment where the chaos needed to be addressed. The company simply had to get on top of itself. Identified was a list of the following needs:

1. Timelines. A production schedule that would be adhered to.

2. Budgeting. Limitation of picture budgets to what had been projected.

3. Planning. Thorough preparation of stories so there would be a minimum of change.

4. Marketing & Sales. A continuing effort to sell and exploit pictures.

5. Accountability. Policing of all departments to prevent unnecessary expenses.

Also identified were the following advantages for doing so, as summarized below:

1. Better product. You can go forward in your desire to make fine pictures with fewer uncertainties and restrictions.

2. Start smarter. You can plan a more specific property-buying program. This is vital because it is where everything starts.

3. Plan better outcomes. We can make long-range distribution, selling, and exploitation plans.

4. Solid financial backing. We can build a sound program for securing new capital and thus strengthen our financial structure.

5. Promises kept. We can meet our financial obligations to the bank and our stockholders.

6. Improved work force culture. We can have a busy, successful, inspired studio which, in turn, means the solution of a thousand and one trivial, yet aggravating problems.

The opportunity to practice these rules was in the production of *Cinderella* itself. Photography and film captured moments to be animated by the artists. But *Cinderella* was a departure in that the entire film was filmed before being animated. Animator Marc Davis in an LA Times article stated it this way:

> You can approach a sequence two ways: You can do it the hard way, which is to start from scratch, animate it out of your head and end up with a first rough," explains Marc Davis, who did much of the animation of the title character in *Cinderella*. "Or you can use the live action to give you that first rough. It also helps to keep the character consistent throughout the film, as one person generally doesn't animate all of a character's scenes.

Thomas' biography reflects also on Walt's work style:

> Walt always had his way around [the studio]. He was the guy, he was just irresistible, and he was so damned right about it. That's why I say, if I contributed anything, I contributed honest management for him. It wasn't that he wasn't smart enough if he applied himself. He was always disinterested in figures, legal work, and all that stuff. It just took time from what he wanted to be thinking about. So, he'd have been easy prey for somebody to twist him and take him.

"Boys, if *Cinderella* doesn't make it, we're through!"

Those were the sentiments of Walt fairly early in the production of *Cinderella*. And that concern continued on until the end of production when he remarked to one magazine editor "The finished picture is not everything that we wanted it to be."

Fortunately, critics—and importantly, movie goers—felt differently. Some saw *Cinderella* as an equal to *Snow White*, if not even better. The film began a new renaissance of animated films to include *Alice in Wonderland*, *Peter Pan*, and *Lady & the Tramp*. Not all were initial box office successes, but like *Cinderella* they have become legendary films of their own time and have delivered tremendous returns. While each cost a few million dollars to make, they have each returned nearly $100 million over the decades, not including merchandising and other revenue streams.

Over the years, *Cinderella* has made well over $250 million in box office sales for the organization. Moreover, *Cinderella*'s success gave Walt the courage to move toward an even bigger project—one that would involve a castle.

Ideas for the Next Century

Consider how you can make the magic come alive for you:

- Where do you have to be "in the weeds" and when do you have to be "above it all" seeing the bigger picture?

- What is your business? How do you balance your avocation or hobby with the need to make a living or build a business?

- Is there a gap between what *you* see as exceeding expectations and what your *customers* see as exceeding expectations? How do you negotiate that gap?

21

A "Treasure Island" of Opportunities

Diversifying Offering and Organization

1950 would be a watershed year for Disney. Not only would it re-emerge as the king of animation with *Cinderella*, but it would begin a new slate of live films that would start the studio moving towards an ongoing production mode. Going into a steady stream of live-action film making allowed the company to diversify its work on two fronts. And yet these films weren't made primarily at the Burbank Studio. They were made in England.

Forcing the Hand into Live-Action Film Work

This all began with film profits being tied up in Europe. The best thing you could do with these monies were to re-invest them in film and production work—particularly in England, which had also created a requirement that 45% of films in British theaters had to be made in England.

So why not take the money that was already there and make some films across the seas?

The first tale of heroism that came alive was the swash buckling *Treasure Island*, released the same year as *Cinderella*. Other than the *True-Life Adventures* and some industrial film efforts, it would be the first Disney film made without any animation being inserted throughout. The benefit was that exterior scenes could be shot in the British countryside and on a real-life schooner from the 19th century. Interiors were filmed at the Denham film studios.

The center of this film was Bobby Driscoll, who played the role of young Jim Hawkins. Bobby had already starred in *Song of the South, So Dear to My Heart*, and a *Pecos Bill* segment of *Melody Time*. Regulations around film production made it difficult for Driscoll to star when he didn't have a valid British work permit. Disney and Driscoll's family were fined and Driscoll ordered to leave the country. During the six weeks it took Disney to prepare an appeal, the director hastily shot all of Driscoll's close-ups, then used his double to shoot the remainder of his shots.

Treasure Island would be followed by *Robin Hood* (1952), *The Sword and the Rose* (1953), and *Rob Roy, The Highland Rogue* (1954). All of these were shot in England and Walt would come back and forth to supervise key aspects of the production.

A Broader Portfolio

Now there wasn't just animation. It wasn't just a choice of full-length animated films or cartoon shorts. There was now a vehicle for making live-action feature films. Add the *True-Life Adventures* documentaries. Then mix in comics, merchandise, Christmas television specials, and more. Even the Ice Capades show offered Disney characters!

Most importantly, much of this didn't require the time or overhead. No matter the format, the films were easier to make than the arduous process of hand-drawn animation. On returning to the Burbank studio after a trip to the United Kingdom, Walt half-jokingly noted: "Those actors over there in England—they're great. You give 'em the lines, they rehearse a couple of times, and you've got it on film—it's finished. You guys take months to draw a scene."

Roy loved all this stating that the new sources of income protected the studio "against the ups and downs of economic conditions, propelled by these new incomes" (and in Roy's mind, more evenly delivered box revenues). Often these kinds of films were placed as double features, perhaps with a Disney animated short as well.

Walt said:

> To some people, I am kind of a Merlin who takes lots of crazy chances, but rarely makes mistakes. I've made some bad ones, but, fortunately, the successes have come along fast enough to cover up the mistakes. When you go to bat as many times as I do, you're bound to get a good average.

Ideas for the Next Century

Consider how you can make the magic come alive for you:

- When doors close, how do you open new windows of opportunity?

- How does diversifying your portfolio help you to hedge against losses?

- How can you build your average for success by getting up to bat more often?

22

20,000 Leagues Under the Sea

Creating a Live-Action Spectacular

An Opportunity to Prove Yourself

Moving into the 1950s, it seemed like the worries of the previous strike and war, as well as all the doldrums of the past decade had moved away. New opportunities awaited. Disney had done animation, nature documentaries and now live action. If these different formats succeeded independently, or alongside as a double-feature, what if these elements could be combined into a huge live-action-adventure film? Walt chose to combine a live-action film in a true-life adventure setting. That 1954 film would be *20,000 Leagues Under the Sea*, based on Jules Verne's epic tale. Curiously, Walt had acquired the film rights for the film thinking that perhaps it would make a great animated film. But now that he had gained experience in live-action film making, he gave up the animation idea and instead created a live-action film. The experience would be filmed in Technicolor and shown in the newly developed CinemaScope.

For the first time, a Disney film would be distributed by Disney, not RKO under the Buena Vista title. To make that succeed, the film had to be marketed as an A film not a B film. B films were seen as more cheaply produced, formulaic films that served as the second feature in a double bill. The double bill began during the Great Depression as a way of getting people to come back into theaters when they had little money: two features, cartoons, a newsreel, and

previews of forthcoming films. Studios were compelled to make them
because many of the studios owned the movie theaters at that time.

Apparently, Walt's idea for making a great A film was to hire a
successful B director. Richard Fleischer won favor with Howard
Hughes while making B films for RKO. Walt chose Richard to step
away from RKO and make *20,000 Leagues* ("*20K*") as an A film,
almost as a statement back to RKO and Hughes that they could not
only distribute a film on their own but take from their own stable to
make a great film to do so. Curiously, Richard was the son of one of
Walt's greatest rivals, Max Fleischer, who headed Fleischer Studios
and created Koko the Clown, Betty Boop, and Popeye. Richard
asked his father for permission to work with Walt. Max told his son
to tell Walt, "he had great taste in directors." His son, Richard, was
so successful directing the *20K* crew, that Kirk Douglas hired him to
make *The Vikings* afterwards.

But the film not only had a tremendous cast with Kirk Douglas,
James Mason, Paul Lukas, and Peter Lorre, but it had the support of
great artists and designers. Harper Goff, who had designed the set
for Warner Brother's *Casablanca*, came in as Art Director for the film.
He and Walt met for the first time in 1951 when both were trying to
purchase the same model train in a London model-making shop.

Production Challenges

- The film work commenced with Harper Goff doing storyboards
  before the film had a script. The book was more episodic rather
  than being one complete story. Making it a "jail break"
  experience for the three men trying to escape prison from the sub
  was the answer for creating a story continuity. Harper would also
  design the Nautilus ship and even give Kirk Douglass lessons on
  how to play a guitar.

- Three studios were used: Disney, Universal, and 20th Century
  Fox. The film then involved distance location shooting in
  Jamaica for the island native warrior scene. Then they filmed in
  the Bahamas for the underwater scenes with divers wearing

105

experimental suits weighing over 150 pounds. The final major filming for the inland island scene took place in Death Valley, California. Some technical scenes were so complex that they involved up to 400 personnel.

• Peter Ellenshaw came in from England to create matte paintings of San Francisco harbor and the inside of the volcano of Vulcania. These were large panes of glass with intricate paintings of difficult-to-recreate scenes. They were brought onto location and overlayed in between the camera and the action being shot, giving the illusion that the performers were in a very different setting.

• To create the illusion of fish swimming outside the portals of the ship and past the divers deep below, an animator spent six months animating fish. But they ended up using much of the footage of fish shot in the Bahamas.

Budgets Strangled by a Squid

The battle with the giant squid was the most difficult and expensive part of the film. Studio 3 was built at Walt Disney Studios for the sole purpose of shooting the scene. The idea was that the *Nautilus* would break the surface in the red after-glow of sunset, the ugly body of the squid silhouetted against the horizon, its long tentacles writhing. From there a fight would ensue with the creature. But the waters were too calm and the squid with its wires looked fake. Walt took a look at the dailies and it to him looked more like a Keystone Cop experience.

Shooting was halted on March 17, 1954, with Walt promising a better squid. The writer saw the dailies and noted that it should take place at night in a violent storm with lightning and waves. The storm, however, added expenses ($250K in 1954), but the reshooting was far more successful. The tentacles were doubled in length; the entire squid weighed in at two tons and involved 28 men to bring it to life.

Cost overruns were happening at the time that Disneyland was costing money. The bankers came in to see the reels and loved it so much they credited them additional funds to finish the picture.

The Result

In total, the film took two years to make: one year to prepare, six months to shoot, and six months to edit. At 2.4 million, the film would be the most expensive film created at the time—even outdoing the cost of *Gone with the Wind*. With all this, Disney marketed the film as "The Mightiest Motion Picture of Them All." Film critic Bosley Crowther would call the film "as fabulous and fantastic as anything he [Disney] has ever done in cartoons."

The first episode of the Disneyland show was a walk-through of Disneyland. But the second show would be "Operation Undersea." If the first episode was a commercial for the new park, the second was likewise an ad to see the film. That episode won Disney an Emmy.

The film was officially released in New York City on December 23, 1954. But it wasn't widely distributed until about the time that Disneyland opened. Curiously, it should be noted that the US Navy launched its first nuclear submarine 21 days after the film premiered. They chose "USS Nautilus" as the name of that sub. Disney would also name one of its submarines in 1959 "Nautilus" as well.

After the completion of the film, the Nautilus set was sent to Disneyland for the opening of the park. Walt was found touching up the paint on portions of the set as the exhibit got ready for opening. The organ's base and keyboard from the Nautilus sub eventually found a home in the ballroom scene of the Haunted Mansion.

The film won two Academy Awards: one for art direction and one for special effects.

In 1957, after searching for topics that would align with Disneyland's Tomorrowland segments, *Our Friend the Atom* was showcased utilizing scenes that highlighted the *20K* sub as an example of a machine powered by a "magical force." It was aligned, at least in principle, to the campaign Dwight D. Eisenhower made around "Atoms for Peace" when he spoke to the UN General Assembly in December of 1993. That short would be transformed into a children's book, as well as into 16 mm movie for classrooms.

When Walt Disney World in Florida opened, the submarine concept from Disneyland was changed to Nautilus-styled submarines in a tropical lagoon. This attraction was wildly popular for years.

After Disneyland Paris opened, they added on a walk-through version of the Nautilus Submarine. Tom Sherman, who was a fan of the film as a child and who had re-done an apartment in the interior of the Nautilus, was hired as an Imagineer to lead the effort.

Tokyo DisneySea created an entire land based on *20,000 Leagues Under the Sea* as the focal point of its park, with a fire-and-smoke-blowing Vulcania at its center and a Nautilus sub in its interior lagoon. A ride-through attraction is also part of that experience.

As The Disney Cruise Line announced in 2023 one of its newest ships, The Disney Treasure, the noted that one of the lounge spaces, Periscope Pub, would be based on 20K. Over 50 years later, this film has continued to inspire across the entire organization.

Ideas for the Next Century

Consider how you can make the magic come alive for you:

- How can you combine all your assets to create the best product or offering?

- How can you give "A talent" opportunities to those who have only had "B talent" options?

- What are the "squids" that try to drown you? When do you have to start over to create something much better?

23

Designing Disneyland

Making a Vision Come Alive

How did the original design come about for what Disneyland would look like? The idea for Disneyland came over many years, if not decades. Even before Walt Disney spent his weekends watching his daughters ride the merry-go-round at the park, he had been exposed to the ideas of parks, expositions, and amusement enterprises. His father's move to Chicago, where Walt was born in 1901, was the result of working on the World's Columbian Exposition of 1893. That resulted in many ideas going back and forth in Walt's mind, to include the Mickey Mouse Park idea next to the studio.

The park idea grew bigger in Walt's mind. Bigger means pricier. He needed to get others to help invest. And while Walt was a master storyteller, this kind of venture would require something visual—especially if it were Roy all alone making the pitch? But who could draw this most unusual map? There are many retellings of this story, which you can find in many places. Here's what we know.

The Right Artist for the Right Time

Artist Herb Ryman was an artist and illustrator who worked for MGM and for 20th Century Fox. This included the Emerald City segment of *The Wizard of Oz*. In 1938, Walt Disney saw an exhibit of Ryman's works at the Chouinard Art Institute and recruited him to come work at Disney. He served as an art director for *Fantasia* and

Dumbo, and then joined the "Good Will Tour of South America" with Walt Disney and the others. He was often one of the only artists invited along with his mother to dinner at the Disney home. But after the war he left the studio to work with 20th Century Fox, being attracted to the opportunity of working on the film, *Anna and the King of Siam.* At one point he took a reprieve from his film work to travel with the Ringling Bros. and Barnum & Bailey Circus documenting the three-ring spectacle with his paintings.

The experience taught Herb how to work with producers, directors, and others to paint a concept of how a scene would be set in a film. In many instances, he had to sketch back quickly what people were describing. In his own words, "I was not a stranger to doing quick sketches."

This offers a framework for how Walt viewed Herb and the kind of talent and insight that Herb had—skills that were different than other artists. While Herb was missing many of the benefits of being a studio employee, he saw himself as having independence in his work. That ability to stand apart, as well as his unique set of skills, set him up for an unusual but pivotal moment not only for him, but for how Disney would face moving forward. It is Saturday morning, September 26, 1953, and Walt Disney calls up Herb. Walt needs a big favor—on a weekend no less—and he seeks an artist that is not on his payroll, even though he has hundreds that are.

In the words of Herb Ryman, here is what was shared on that call:

> The telephone rang and it was Walt and he said, "Hi, Herbie, what are you doing?" And I said I'm working on my circus paintings. And he said, "Well, could you come over and see me?" And I said, where are you? And he said, "Well, I'm at the studio." And I said: You're working on Saturday? And he said, "Yes—I can work on Saturday or Sunday, or anything I want. It's my studio!"

> And of course, it was. So, I was curious why Walt would want to see me? And he said "Herbie, I'm going to do an amusement park." I said: Well now, what do you want to talk

to me about? He said, "Herbie, my brother Roy has got to go to New York on Monday, has got to fly to New York. We need 17 million dollars to start this project. Roy has to take this stuff back and show them what this is going to look like."

And so, I got excited and said: Well, I would like to see it too. And he said, "You're going to do it!"

This context sets the stage for what would happen next. Herb showered and headed over to the studio where for some 42 hours Walt talked and Herb Ryman drew. Herb made clear his expectations that Walt would stay with him the entire time. And Walt did. In Neil Gabler's version of this story in Walt's life, he wrote:

> Ryman immediately objected. He was afraid he would embarrass himself with so little time. "Walt paced back and forth," Ryman recalled. "Then he went over into the corner, and he turned his head around with his back to me and said coaxingly, 'Will you do it if I stay here with you?'" Ryman didn't see how that would necessarily help, but Walt was so plaintive—"like a little boy," he said in one interview, "with tears in his eyes," he said in another—that Ryman reluctantly agreed. Plied with tuna sandwiches and milkshakes and coached by Walt, who provided detailed descriptions and chain-smoked, Ryman worked straight through Sunday, sleepless, forty-two hours in all by one account.

As an example, Herb shared Walt's vision of the importance of a central hub and of how the guests would move through the experience. This is how Walt explained it to Herb:

> You know, he said, when I was in Europe, when I was studying this thing he said, "One of the great problems with amusement parks—any kind of a park—is that people, they get exhausted walking." Now he said: "I want to have these radiating spokes from the hub so that people that are tired, or sick or old, or they can say, well you kids run on ahead, we'll meet you there in 45 minutes."

And there again was the secret of Walt's amazing concept of entertainment. He knew people had to be comfortable.

When Dick Irvine and Marvin Davis showed up for work on Monday, Walt and Herb were still there, exhausted, but finished. The result was colored by Marv Davis and Dick Irvine and air-mailed to Roy in New York. The drawing would play a major role in getting the board at ABC to eventually create a deal with Walt and Roy for building Disneyland. This time, Roy wasn't visiting the banks. He was visiting the television networks.

At one point Herb said to Walt, "I'll work on this thing as long as it's interesting and exciting. And when it ceases to be interesting, I'll go back to my work. And Walt said, and I remember very well, Well Herbie, I'll try to make it interesting. And of course, he did." In the end, Herb Ryman went on to make a huge contribution to Disney Imagineering in the decades that followed. From Walt Disney World to Epcot to Tokyo Disneyland.

Beyond this, however, there was something about working with Walt Disney that was simply an honor in and of itself. Herb Ryman observed: "There was just something about him that made you want to please him...and gaining his confidence was better than payday."

Ideas for the Next Century

Consider how you can make the magic come alive for you:

- Are you agile enough to stop and make something come to life for others?

- If you could paint one picture of your vision, what would it look like?

- Can you paint a vision that will get others on board with what you want to accomplish?

24

Entering Television & ABC

New Risks & Partnerships

Television was on Walt's mind for many years. When *Snow White and the Seven Dwarfs* premiered, it was done through RKO Pictures. Previously, all Disney films had been distributed by United Artists, but a new contract proposed by United Artists during that early era required that Disney sign away television rights to its films. "I don't know what television is," Walt argued, "but I'm not going to sign away anything I don't know about." Walt signed with RKO instead.

The Smallest Film Studio and the Smallest Television Network Team Together

Of course, the Disney Company has owned ABC television since 1996. And many baby boomers know that Disney and ABC go back many, many decades. But few know what a risk or how unusual it was for a movie studio, much less an animation studio, to become involved with television.

To describe ABC television in the early 1950s as a second-rate network to powerhouses CBS and NBC is to give it a compliment. ABC wasn't even in the same league as the two other networks. In the context of the cold war, comedian Milton Berle stated: "In case they [the Soviets] drop the big bomb, go to ABC; they've never had a hit!"

So, it was very courageous and innovative that Walt Disney chose to be the first studio producer to venture into the unknown world of television. This venture began with two holiday specials for the bigger networks, that were well-received by the public. First was the 1950 Christmas special, "One Hour in Wonderland" for NBC. Then in 1951 came "Walt Disney Christmas Show" for CBS. But conversations with the networks about a television series would bog down in part because Walt would talk about building a park, when networks were trying to create TV shows. Even Roy was perplexed, calling it "another one of Walt's screwy ideas."

Going back and forth and unable to get the television networks to invest in his Disneyland project, Walt and Roy eventually struck a deal to create television programming for ABC. That was in large part because of the drawing Herb Ryman created. The map not only provided a visual way to make understanding easier to grasp, but it also mapped out a formula for Disney for years to come. The show, *Disneyland*, would outline the different realms of the park. Walt would use *True-Life Adventure* footage for Adventureland. In Fantasyland, he would showcase cartoon shorts and animated films created over the decades. Frontierland would underscore the country's fascination of the American west with heroes like Davy Crockett. And Tomorrowland would demonstrate possibilities about the future.

Even with the image Ryman had created it would take many more months before the complicated arrangement was finalized. Beyond the inherent risks in such an arrangement, the deal between Disney and ABC blew away Hollywood. Most studio and theater owners considered television as a threat to their very existence. Stars on contract with the studios were not allowed to appear on television. Indeed, most television programming was done in New York, not in California. The studios didn't even like televisions to appear in their films. Walt saw it differently: "Instead of considering TV a rival, when I saw it, I said, 'I can use that. I want to be part of it.'"

Combining a Theme Park with Television

Walt had a grander vision of what his shows could do on ABC, and how they could be used to promote Disneyland. Despite pressure from the other studios, Walt and Roy signed a contract with Leonard Goldenson of ABC, in which the network would put up $500,000 in cash, guarantee $4.5 million in loans, and receive one-third ownership in Disneyland (which it later sold back to Disney).

Walt Disney Productions made a public announcement on April 2, 1954, that Disney would provide the ABC network with "an entirely new concept in television programming." On May 1, 1954, they announced that they would be building an amusement park. Eventually, other shows were introduced on ABC to include *The Mickey Mouse Club* and *Zorro*. The *Mickey Mouse Club* re-invented children's television with a set of Mouseketeers who entertained five days a week. Not only did it put Mickey front and center, but it also created a star of Annette Funicello and other kids who went on to successful careers, both in that show and subsequent versions over the decades. *The Mickey Mouse Club* created the evergreen love of a set of "mouse ears." But that wasn't the only head gear that came out of this arrangement. Davy Crockett was so popular, coonskin caps sold right off the shelf. ABC kept wanting more Westerns, and Disney ultimately delivered with *Zorro*.

The *Disneyland* show was a tremendous success for ABC. For three years it was the only ABC show in the top 15 rated programs. It would make Walt's face as famous as his name; his lead-ins provided an opportunity for him to talk directly to his audience in a tone that was natural and familiar, and which made him a favorite guest in millions of homes. He was to millions, Uncle Walt. It also introduced the world to Disneyland and encouraged them to visit.

And visit they did.

Ideas for the Next Century

Consider how you can make the magic come alive for you:

- What's the last new idea you acted upon?

- Do you look outward for fresh ideas?

- Do you question the status quo or paradigms that your industry has established?

- How can you create synergy with others? How can you combine ideas?

- What new opportunities are out there that you haven't taken advantage of?

25

Disneyland's Opening

Learning from Day One

"Black Sunday"

On July 17, 1955, Walt Disney dedicated Disneyland before a television audience of millions. It was very much the televised event that committed him to opening on that date. While Walt had spent years dreaming up the concept, construction began less than a year earlier, and by opening day, challenges were real. Guests waited in line at Disneyland. They waited in line for food. They waited in line for merchandise. They waited in line to go on rides. They waited in line to get into the park. They even waited so long just to get into the parking lot that first day that some of them were taking a bathroom break on the streets of Anaheim waiting to get in! When news of such came to Roy O. Disney's attention, he smiled, and exclaimed: "Let 'em pee!"

The newly poured asphalt melted, causing the heels of women's shoes to get stuck, and a plumbers' strike kept drinking fountains from being installed in time. And this on a day where the temperature was over 100 degrees Fahrenheit. Critics blasted it as "Black Sunday." Meanwhile, forged tickets were bringing thousands of people into the park without the organization's knowledge.

Learning from One's Mistakes

One such example of Disneyland's opening day challenges was the steamship, *Mark Twain*. This steamship was inspired by many like it that sailed before her down the Mississippi. They were beautiful, but fragile ships. With all of its intricate lattice, one had to be careful not to ground her on the river (hence the depth calls of "Mark One" and "Mark Twain"). One also had to be careful of boilers overheating, blowing up, and resulting in a fatal calamity.

By the time this replica of a steamboat opened with Disneyland on July 17, 1955, those sorts of concerns had long been resolved. But there were still other problems to be encountered. Cast Member Terry O'Brien was one of the first Cast Members hired at that time. Observing all the excitement of that opening day with its parades and celebrities like Art Linkletter and Ronald Reagan, it was easy to be distracted and make a mistake.

O'Brien's role was to admit Guests into the holding area where they would await the next ship. Since the ship was brand new, they really had no idea how many to admit at one time onto the ship. The designers estimated the number should be kept around 200-300. With no turnstile, Terry was given a clicker, and all day he would click as people entered into the holding area.

After a while, the job became mundane, so O'Brien started chatting with Guests. The ship came into the landing and another group took off. Shortly afterwards, the ship signaled trouble. With so many Guests on board, the boat had derailed off the track and sunk into the mud. It took a while for management to get it fixed and back on the rail. As it came back to the landing, all the people rushed to the side to get off, and the boat tipped into the water again.

The supervisor approached Terry O'Brien and asked how many people he'd put on the boat. Quickly, Terry responded "about 250," to which the supervisor suggested that it stay at around 200. As the supervisor left, Terry took a look at the clicker and realized that he had actually put 508 passengers aboard the Mark Twain. Embarrassed, he told no one. Terry made sure that it never happened again.

Terry wasn't the only one learning that day. No one had ever created something like Disneyland, and it would take a long time to learn what was needed to make it successful. The reality is everyone makes mistakes, and we must create a learning culture so that people learn from those mistakes. When we don't allow people to make mistakes and learn from them, they tend to go underground. Much preferred is an organization that permits people to identify lessons from their mistakes and to use them as opportunities for improving the organization.

All that said, Leslie Iwerks (granddaughter of Ub Iwerks) wrote in *The Imagineering Story* that on the day after, when the paying public was first admitted, people started lining up at 2:00 am. The freeways would eventually jam up like the day before, and by the 10 a.m. opening there were some 6,000 in line. Over a million customers showed up in the first two months, and 3.5 million came in the first year. Whatever "Black Sunday" pain they experienced on the opening day press event, was now "Green Monday" for bringing in the dollars. Disneyland never looked back as it became, in Imagineer John Hench's mind, the greatest Disney accomplishment.

Ideas for the Next Century

Consider how you can make the magic come alive for you:

- Is your organization a learning culture? Do you allow people to learn from their mistakes, or do you hold it against them?

- What can you do to send a message that people should not only learn from their mistakes, but share them to the benefit of others?

- How do you turn your "Black Sundays" into "Green Mondays"?

26

Space in Tomorrowland

Painting the Future

What's Happening Tomorrow?

One of the biggest challenges getting Disneyland opened was the building of Tomorrowland. And it wasn't just the space to the right of the hub. *Disneyland* the TV show had promised shows on the future and figuring that out became its own dilemma. Originally when Walt Disney was considering the topics to include for his "Tomorrowland" segment of *Disneyland* this history of the wheel was addressed in an early storyboard meeting as the first topic. Not surprising, since one of the first attractions to pen would be based on the cars of "Autopia." Writer Charles Shows, hired to write for the series, said that in a storyboard meeting Walt Disney asked him how he felt about such a topic. In his words:

> I was caught by surprise. I had not expected him to ask my opinion... "The invention of the wheel is yesterday's story," I heard myself declare "Today the big story is space—space travel"...I had brought with me the new issue of *Life* magazine that I had bought that morning. The cover of *Life* featured a drawing of a dramatic new space rocket designed by Werner von Braun. It was designed, the article said, to land American astronauts on the moon in just a few years. The prospect was phenomenal. Nervously, I leaned forward and handed the magazine to Walt.

For the next ten minutes, all of us sat in rapt silence as Walt carefully read the entire article. Finally, he looked up at us.

"Do you realize," he said incredulously, "that this von Braun—the same guy who developed the German V-2 rocket—has perfected a new rocket—to land men on the moon, in just a few years?" A loud murmur went through the room. Everyone promptly forgot the wheel story. At that moment Walt Disney entered the Age of Space.

A Free Hand in Space

At first, ABC gave Walt Disney a free hand in production. Because Walt was very busy with Disneyland, he in turn gave his people a free hand. For Ward Kimball, producer of the *Man in Space* series, this also included a blank check. Kimball noted that Walt himself directed: "Write your own ticket." Bill Bosche, an associate to the project commented on such a statement: "I remember Harry Tytle [a chief animator] was standing there when Walt said that, and his eyes just about dropped out of his head. Walt never said anything like that." According to Scholer Bangs of the *Los Angeles Herald and Express* the time spent in pre-production on models and illustrations paid off in *Man in Space*:

> Walt Disney may be America's "Secret Weapon" for the conquest of space! Apparently and quite by accident he has discovered the "trigger" that may blast loose his country's financial resources and place the Stars and Stripes of the United States aboard the first inhabited earth satellite. Disney's immediate achievement, with the aid of this triumvirate of space authorities, is the suggestion that space travel no longer is a wild dream; that it is so near we can practically feel the earth tremble under the rocket blast of Dr. von Braun's spaceship. *Man in Space* is believable, and Disney has close to 100,000,000 Americans believing. Half of the voting population of the USA has probably reached two impressive conclusions: "It CAN be done!" and "Let's get on with it!"

Apparently, President Dwight D. Eisenhower was so impressed with the first installment of the series, he called Walt Disney and requested that it be shown to officials at the Pentagon. After the loss of the U.S. space race in 1957, the American leadership agreed to Werner von Braun's critical role in the design of space rockets.

Perhaps no greater credit was given to the authenticity of the series than from von Braun himself the day Apollo 8 first circled the moon. In his thick German accent, he called up Ward Kimball and told him: "Well Wahd, it looks like they're following our script."

Ideas for the Next Century

Consider how you can make the magic come alive for you:

- Do you know what tomorrow looks like? Can you paint a picture of the possibilities?

- Do you have a culture where people feel free to share their ideas, or express their opinions?

- What would it take to create a place where people can bring new insight to the table?

- How do you need to do to give people a "free hand" to do what they need to succeed?

27

"We Create Happiness"

The Power of a Service Mantra

Pointing Everyone in the Same Direction

Imagine you could have any role at Disneyland...What job would you want?

You could be a conductor on *The Disneyland Railroad*, pick up trash, sail rafts across the Rivers of America, or paddle canoes. You could be "best friends" with Mickey Mouse, or wave to others in the parade as a princess. You could be an Imagineer, or even the President of the entire Walt Disney Company. No matter what job you choose, even if you are the new CEO of the Walt Disney Company, you will attend a classroom orientation known as "Disney Traditions." During this orientation you will learn the mission of the company and what your number one priority is. That priority can be stated in just three words:

We Create Happiness.

That's what it was in 1955 when Dick Nunis and Van France created "Disney Traditions." The mission is a little longer now. In 1971 it was changed to: "We create happiness by providing the finest in entertainment."

It changed again in 1990: "We create happiness by providing the finest in entertainment to people of all ages everywhere."

But when you're teaching an 18-year-old Cast Member what their job is, it's easier to say simply, "We create happiness." The power of this is that while everyone may not remember everything shared on the first day of an orientation, everyone should walk away with three words "We create happiness."

"We Create Happiness," a concept built by Dick and Van when Disneyland was first created, has endured until today. By shaping a vision in your own organization, you can build an ideal, a statement, that exemplifies the products and services you offer. In their landmark book *In Search of Excellence*, Tom Peters and Robert Waterman wrote:

> "Whether or not they are as fanatical in their service obsession as Frito, IBM, or Disney, the excellent companies all seem to have very powerful service themes that pervade the institutions. In fact, one of our most significant conclusions is that, whether their basic business is metal-bending, high technology, or hamburgers, they have all defined themselves as service businesses."

Making Happiness Operational

Imagine the possibilities, even the power, when everyone is pointed in the same direction with the same higher purpose in mind! It's attainable even in your kingdom, just as it is in this happiest of all places. Here is how a vision like "creating happiness" becomes operational in a place like Disney:

One day, a Jungle Cruise pilot failed to notice that Walt Disney himself had joined the fellow passengers. In the early days of Disneyland, Walt would frequently stroll through the park, observing the Guest experience by simply walking around. When the cruise was over, Walt stepped off the boat and walked up to the one of the park's superintendents, Dick Nunis. "Dick, what's the trip time on this ride?" Nunis replied that it was seven minutes. "I just got a four and-a-half-minute trip. How would you like to go to a movie and have the theater remove a reel in the middle of the picture?" Walt Disney continued, "Do you realize how much those hippos cost? I want people to see them, not be rushed through a ride by some guy who's bored with his work."

"Could I go on a trip with you?" Dick Nunis asked. Walt agreed to it. So, Dick and Walt rode one of the boats through Adventureland and Walt demonstrated how to navigate the experience— "Speed up in the dull stretches, then slow down when you have something to look at." Walt modeled what he expected of others. He demonstrated what the perfect voyage would look like.

For a full week thereafter, the Jungle Cruise pilots were timed with stopwatches until they perfected the length of the ride. When Walt arrived for his regular visit to Disneyland on a subsequent weekend, he walked through Adventureland without stopping for a ride. He did the same the following weekend.

After three weeks, he took a ride on one of the boats. When he returned to the dock, he entered the next boat for another ride. He went around four times, eliminating the possibility that the operators had "stacked the deck" by giving him the best pilots. When he emerged from the fourth trip, he turned to Dick Nunis and gave him a thumbs-up sign.

Since then, that thumbs-up sign has come to represent "great show" in providing Guest service in all the Disney parks. Recognition— even as simple as giving a thumbs up—is part of what creates a great service culture. So is training others. So is modeling the correct behavior. So is walking the park. All of these elements combine to elevate the customer experience. Only at Disney, they wouldn't be customers. They would be Guests.

Ideas for the Next Century

Consider how you can make the magic come alive for you:

- Do you have a succinct declaration of your organization's purpose? Does it create an image of your organization?

- Is your mission more than a corporate mission statement nailed to the wall in some boardroom?

- Is everyone on board—agree—with that mission? How will you get co-workers on board with the mission?

- How does your role tie into the mission of the organization?

- How do you operationalize your organization's purpose?

28

The Disneyland Hotel

Building Partnerships

It took all of Walt's financial resources to make Disneyland a reality. Yet he knew that there was a need to provide for people who were coming from across the country to visit Disneyland. The surrounding area of 1955 Anaheim offered little if anything in terms of accommodations for those needing a place to stay. The need for a hotel opportunity was critical, and no one knew that more than Walt, who himself had an apartment built above the firehouse on Main Street USA, for nights and weekends when he came out to the park.

Jack Wrather was a Texas oil man who had already established himself in Hollywood with television hits like *Lassie* and *The Lone Ranger*, as well as ownership in television and radio stations. Moreover, he had become involved with hotels in Las Vegas and Palm Springs. As his neighbors, Walt approached Jack and his wife Bonita about building a hotel adjacent to Disneyland. Walt was even willing to give him the rights to use the name "Disney" not only in building that hotel, but any other he might build in the United States.

Catering to a Different Audience

The first challenge was to build the hotel when all of the available construction crews were dedicated to building Disneyland. Therefore, the hotel didn't open until October 5, 1955, and at that,

A CENTURY OF POWERFUL DISNEY INSIGHTS

there were only 7 rooms available on opening day. While the idea of roadside motels like Holiday Inn accommodated families, the hotel business itself was tailored to businessmen on the road. The Disneyland Hotel really thought about families and catered to aspects of their experience. As a resort, this would eventually include amenities unlike any other. Spacious rooms were established that could house families staying the night.

All this was in part to provide for and attract guests to stay in their hotel even on days and nights when Disneyland was not open to the public, as it closed during the off season, two days a week.

Amenities Worthy of Its World-Class Neighbor

To make it a resort destination in and of itself, the following were part of the Disneyland Resort Hotel offerings over the years:

- Rooms with soundproof air walls
- Color televisions—the first hotel ever to offer them
- A retail shopping arcade
- Casual and formal restaurants and lounges
- Convention and meeting space—first for Orange County
- 9-Hole Golf Course
- Tennis Court
- Full-size Olympic pool
- Casual play pool with a tropical tide pool and white sand beaches
- Arcades for video games and remote miniature boats & cars for steering
- Aqua Gardens, reflecting pools, waterfall features, & koi fish grotto
- Beauty salons and barber shops
- Radio station
- Indoor/outdoor nurseries for children with trained nurses
- Dormitory style accommodations for organized youth groups, clubs, and children's organizations
- Helicopter pad with access to Los Angeles International Airport
- Miniature golf course designed to Disneyland attractions

128

- Marina—including not only paddle boats for rent but actual watercraft for sale
- Fantasy Water show (a precursor to what would inspire World of Color)
- An adjacent recreational vehicle park known as Vacationland

But the best amenity of all was the Disneyland monorail. A shorter course was established in 1959, but Walt saw the possibilities of linking track all the way out to the hotel and back. This set Disneyland Hotel in a category all by itself even beyond the name it held. With that success, towers were added to the property (Bonita, Marina, and Sierra). By 1960, there were 300 rooms, and the hotel was the largest in Orange County, California.

A Template for Future Disney Hotels

After Walt Disney's death, the Walt Disney organization began making overtures to purchase the hotel. After the passing of Jack and Bonita, Disney purchased the entire Wrather Corporation in 1988, acquiring not only the Disneyland Hotel, but the lease to operate the Queen Mary, which Jack had acquired earlier as well. This created the possibility of building an ocean-themed park in the Long Beach area, which ultimately never happened. But the ideas would evolve into what became known as Tokyo DisneySea in Tokyo. Many of the original buildings of the Disneyland Hotel were torn down and rebuilt to serve as an anchor to Downtown Disney when it eventually opened in 2001. But that also became an additional link between the Disneyland Hotel and the rest of the Disneyland Resort

Most importantly, the vision and investment Jack and Bonita Wrather had for this hotel became the template for resort hotels the company would create in the years to come. The Polynesian took cues from the original garden-style wings found in the original Disneyland Hotel. The Contemporary also did the same and then added the tower. Both had the benefit of a monorail passing by, and in the latter instance, actually going through it. Even Vacationland would be a precursor to Disney's Fort Wilderness Resort &

Campground. And all provided spaces and amenities that would appeal to families staying and visiting Disney.

Ideas for the Next Century

Consider how you can make the magic come alive for you:

- Does your name and reputation speak value and quality? If you were to buy back your name, what would it be worth?

- How do you cater to your core audience? How is that different from others in your industry?

- How do your offerings and amenities present you as a complete offering or experience?

29

More than an Amusement Park

The Customer Experience at Disneyland

Before Disneyland was built, Walt would take his daughters to the park and watch them on the merry-go-round. As he sat there eating peanuts, he would think about how there must be some enterprise that could be built so that both parents and children could enjoy the experience together.

A Carousel, not a Merry-Go-Round

Actually, the technical difference between the two words is the direction they go in. A Merry-Go-Round turns clockwise, while a Carousel in the United States turns counterclockwise. But there's another different sense to these two words. One seems more than just an amusement park. And so, it's not surprising that Disneyland would call it King Arthur Carousel, an attraction that was there from opening day.

It's actually the park's oldest attraction, having been handcrafted by the Dentzel Carousel Company in Philadelphia, Pennsylvania, and was in use in Sunnyside Beach Park, Toronto, Canada, by 1922. It originally included giraffes, deer, and other animals but Walt wanted everyone to ride a galloping horse going up and down like King Arthur. So other horses were acquired, and another row or "course" was added allowing for 71 horses to reside at any time. Backup horses would be on hand so that they could be rotated in and out for refurbishment. Gold and silver paint would complement the details of the horses. Cleaning the brass poles would require the entire time of an individual during the third hour shift. And 3,328 lights would be kept in working order.

Did Walt accomplish his objective? Perhaps that could be answered in part by this guest letter that Disneyland used for many years as a training tool. The author, a Mr. Schuch, supervised American Airlines ticket agents and baggage handlers and wrote the letter to inspire his own employees.

American Airlines, Inc.

December 6, 1957
To: All Terminal Service Personnel
From: Superintendent-Terminal Service — LAX
Subject: Customer Service

"I recently broke down and finally agreed to take my family on an outing to Walt Disney's Magic Kingdom—Disneyland. Many of you have already been there and no doubt have made the same observations that I am going to talk about, but I thought some of you might be interested in the marvelous reaction that my family received from this visit.

"...My two daughters, ages 3 and 5, made a beeline for Fantasyland and surprised me by heading for the cheapest ride in the park—a ten-cent whirl on King Arthur Carousel. We noticed that every attendant was in immaculate uniform. They took charge of our kiddies at the entrance, placed them on their horses, strapped them on, and gave them a big reassuring smile. After they rode in circles for several minutes, the same attendants gave them another big smile, helped them down, and gave each one a little pat on the back as they left. My oldest daughter made this comment, "I don't want to ride on the merry-go-round at Redondo Beach anymore, daddy, because the man there isn't as nice as that man." Here is service having an impact on a five-year old, but Walt Disney's standards are high, and ten cents is still a piece of revenue."

Mr. Schuch goes on to discuss an experience in Storybook Land as well as how clean the park is. He then concludes by saying:

"All of this might sound corny, and it also might convey the thought I have a sideline job as one of Disney's public relations representatives. This, of course, is not true. His Magic Kingdom impressed us so much that I could not help comparing his operation with that of American Airlines. His standards of service must be extremely high. He must screen and re-screen every employee that applies for a job. There must be a constant inspection activity going on, otherwise, his domain would not present such an appearance or his employees would not offer such outstanding service.

"We were impressed—not just with the fantasy, the splashes of vivid color, or the immensity of the operation; No—this didn't impress us half as much as the things that are outlined above.

"We will all go back to Disneyland—the service is terrific.

"O. A. Schuch"

Service today is defined somewhat differently than it was then. Mr. Schuch described it back in 1957. Still, the foundations are important. Whether it's maintaining a great product, or offering attentive 1:1 service, or at best, a great total experience.

Ideas for the Next Century

Consider how you can make the magic come alive for you:

- What are the foundations of great customer service that make your organization succeed?

- How do you attend to those details and to keeping them up?

- How does the application of those foundations evolve over time?

30

Mary Poppins

Making Something Supercalifragilisticexpialidocious

The Search for Something Practically Perfect

People may pay good money for good entertainment, but finding the right story is often not easy. Walt Disney was always searching for the next great tale. One such opportunity occurred in 1944, when he went to his daughter's bedside to tuck her in and saw a book called *Mary Poppins*. "What's this?" he asked her. "You should read it, Daddy, it could be a movie." Walt took her advice, but he ran into an obstacle: the author, P. L. Travers. She wanted nothing to do with Hollywood or with Walt Disney.

Over the next several years, whenever Walt was in Europe to make films like *Treasure Island* or to Zermat, Switzerland, to film *Third Man on the Mountain*—he would visit Travers, charming her and sharing his ideas for a *Mary Poppins* film. It took 16 years, but she finally gave in. But that was only half the victory; now that Walt had his story, he needed to find the right people to bring it to life.

Combining Everything You Do Best

In the years prior to *Mary Poppins*, Walt had been more involved with Disneyland than his films. That changed with *Mary Poppins*: Walt was involved with every aspect of the movie, and his personal touch is evident. For example, he added the sidewalk chalk painting fantasy sequence, the one-man band, and the iconic chimney sweep dance over the rooftops. In the film tribute to Walt shown at *One Man's Dream* in Hollywood Studios (and hosted by Julie Andrews), Walt explains:

> After a long concentration on live-action and cartoon films, we decided to try something that would employ about every trick we learned in the making of films. We would combine cartoon and live-action in an enormous fantasy—*Mary Poppins*. And what a far cry that was from *Snow White*. As the original *Mary Poppins* budget of five million dollars continued to grow, I never saw a sad face around the entire Studio. And this made me nervous. I knew the picture would have to gross 10 million dollars for us to break even. But there was no negative head shaking. No prophets of doom. Roy was so happy he didn't even ask me to show the unfinished picture to a banker. The horrible thought struck me—suppose the staff had finally conceded that I knew what I was doing?

Casting the character of Mary Poppins, who in the books is frumpy, much like her creator, was difficult. Bette Davis, Walt's first choice, was unavailable, so he decided to change course and look for a younger, more attractive actress. His secretary suggested Julie Andrews, the star of Broadway's *My Fair Lady*. After watching her perform in *Camelot*, Walt knew he'd found his Mary Poppins. Andrews, however, was in the running to star in the film version of *My Fair Lady*. When Jack Warner rejected her for that role, saying she was not photogenic, Andrews took Walt's offer.

The studio staff's impression of *Mary Poppins* can be explained by the word, "Supercalifragilisticexpialidocious." This word is a form of double-talk, intended to say something important when you have nothing to say. The Sherman Brothers, Richard and Robert, remembered the word from their childhood, and it suits the film perfectly because it appears that even the staff had nothing to criticize or say about the production of *Mary Poppins*. Hence, when you have nothing to say, all you can say is Supercalifragilisticexpialidocious!

The film premiere on August 27, 1964, was a grand one, hosted at Grauman's Chinese Theater. The premiere was a benefit for the development of CalArts. Already cast as Bert, Dick Van Dyke sought to also play the role of Mr. Dawes Sr., the oldest banker in the film. He approached Walt, who agreed, with the caveat that Van Dyke donate $4,000 to CalArts. As the final credits roll, you can see that Dick Van Dyke was listed in the role as "Navckid Keyd," an anagram of his name, Dick Van Dyke.

Some two decades after he had first read the book, Walt Disney's long perseverance paid off, critically and financially, for *Mary Poppins* was his greatest film success. The movie won five Academy Awards. And while it lost to *My Fair Lady* in the Best Picture category, Julie Andrews won above Audrey Hepburn for Best Actress.

Ideas for the Next Century

Consider how you can make the magic come alive for you:

- What do you do that is worth paying more than one would expect?

- When people doubt you, why?

- How do you make things so supercalifragilisticexpialidocious they don't doubt you?

- How long must you persist so as to make something supercalifragilisticexpialidocious?

31

A Permanent School for Artists

Investing Long-Term in Your Legacy

With the profits from *Mary Poppins*, Walt focused on funding two major goals in the last years of his life. One was Project X (more on that later). The second was CalArts, a place where a new generation of artists could be trained. This would be a complete community where artists could not only master their field of study but collaborate across conventional categories to conjure new artistic expressions. It would be a permanent gift that would always create a new tomorrow of artists.

Paying Forward to the Future

In the earliest days, Walt would drive artists to school so they could improve. The years passed between *Snow White* and *Mary Poppins*, but Walt's passion and interest in developing the talent of his staff remained strong. So, it was no surprise that one of Walt Disney's last dreams was the creation of a campus for the fine arts. In 1961, Walt and Roy guided the merger of the Chouinard Art Institute and the Los Angeles Conservatory of Music to establish California Institute of the Arts—or CalArts. Walt didn't live to see the actual campus, though he did provide an endowment of half his estate (more than $40 million). His brother Roy took over where he had left off, in addition to guiding the development of the new theme park in Florida. Together they paid forward to the future.

CalArts opened the doors of its temporary campus in 1970, then a year later moved to its permanent campus in Valencia. A key part of the curriculum was the new animation program. "When classes started, it dawned on me pretty quickly how special this was," said John Lasseter, a one-time student who went on to lead Pixar and the Walt Disney Animation Studios. The CalArts faculty included great artists like Ken O'Connor, Jack Hanna, and T. Hee.

In addition to Lasseter, some of the students became influential in their own right, including:

- John Musker, director of *The Little Mermaid*, *Aladdin*, and *The Princess and the Frog*
- Tim Burton, director of *The Nightmare Before Christmas*, and director of *Alice in Wonderland* and *Frankenweenie*
- Chris Buck, co-director of *Tarzan* and *Frozen*
- Brad Bird, director of *The Iron Giant*, *The Incredibles*, and *Ratatouille*
- Michael Giaimo, art director of *Pocahontas* and *Frozen*
- Gary Trousdale, director of *Beauty and the Beast* and *The Hunchback of Notre Dame*
- Henry Selick, director of *Coraline*, *The Nightmare Before Christmas*, and *James and the Giant Beach*

Embracing the Mis-Fit Toys

Early on these individuals were geeky art and film nerds wanting to do what they loved most. In a way, CalArts was like the Island of Mis-Fit Toys. Tim Burton would refer to the early CalArts students as a "collection of outcasts." Roy O. Disney might agree. The "outcasts" attended college during Vietnam, Haight-Ashbury, and Flower Power. Roy did not appreciate news of nude swimming in the campus pool, nor other reports of nudity at CalArts. Bob Thomas, in *Walt Disney: An American Original*, wrote about the reaction of one member of the CalArts board of directors to the complaints about nudity:

> What is wrong with viewing the human body?" [the board member asked]. And then began removing his coat, shirt,

138

shoes, pants, and undershorts in front of the full board, to include Roy himself. One man serving as chairman and school dean gazed at the naked individual, commenting, "What have you got to be so proud of yourself?

There may not have been much to be proud of in those early days of CalArts, but the college survived the 60s and 70s, and continues today as a private university. To date, the students in the Cal Arts animation program have generated $50 billion in box office revenue and were largely responsible for the creation of Pixar and for the re-invention of Disney itself, with two renaissances of Disney Feature Animation.

Walt's vision of education not only created a new institute of learning, but it also made his studio one of the greatest entertainment companies in history. Walt noted: "CalArts is the principal thing I hope to leave when I move on to greener pastures. If I can help provide a place to develop the talent of the future, I think I will have accomplished something."

Ideas for the Next Century

Consider how you can make the magic come alive for you:

- What value is an education to fulfilling your dreams?

- What do you have to be proud of?

- Why is it important is it that you develop your staff?

- How do you demonstrate the importance of developing others?

- How will you leave a lasting legacy? How can you pay forward the future for others?

32

The New York World's Fair

Collaborating for a Win/Win

Electronic Bird Brain Ideas

Through Disneyland Walt Disney had emerged as a Master Showman. Dignitaries and celebrities would come from the world over to visit "The Happiest Place on Earth." Since its opening, he continually re-invested in new attractions such as the Matterhorn Bobsleds, the Submarine Voyage, and the Disneyland Monorail in 1959. In 1963 he introduced a form of animation that would come alive in what was known as The Enchanted Tiki Room. The animation of inanimate objects like hippos, bears, and squids were already a part of the Disneyland landscape originating in 1955. But this new "space age" technology allowed inanimate characters to perform on cue—and even talk. Suddenly Tiki birds, flowers, and totems came to life.

But the Tiki Room was only a test for what Disney had in mind. Back in 1960, Walt gathered his executive at WED, an earlier name he had given to Imagineering that was based on his initials, Walter Elias Disney. Imagineering was about imagination and engineering combined.

> There's going to be a big fair up in New York. All the big corporations in the country are going to be spending a helluva lot of money building exhibits there. They won't know what they want to do. They won't even know why

140

they're doing it, except that the other corporations are doing it and they have to keep up with the Joneses.

They went to work. This is the story of three of the four projects.

General Electric's Progressland

The work with General Electric (GE) actually pre-dates the Fair, when a concept known as Edison Square was being envisioned as an extension of Main Street USA in Disneyland. By 1959, GE was already making requests for help with the New York World's Fair. This pavilion had several pieces to it, but the centerpiece was The Carousel of Progress. This attraction involved Walt personally, as he configured this traveling theater show to be akin to Thornton Wilder's *Our Town*. It would play to the 1880s, the 1920s, the 1940s, and finally the present day 1960's. Complimenting this was a song that would be written by the Sherman Brothers, "A Great Big Beautiful Tomorrow."

In Richard Sherman's mind, the song's strength was its "wonderful positiveness in a way. It was Walt's theme song, because he was very positive about the future. He really did believe that there was a 'Great Big Beautiful Tomorrow' shining at the end of every day."

The show highlighted Disney's animatronic figures, who brought the family to life in each scene. To understand how amazing these robotic-like creatures were, consider the plight of the John F. Kennedy family who visited Progressland at the New York World's Fair without their father after his assassination. In each act of the show there is a dog that is part of the family. The dog seemed so real to then seven-year-old Caroline Kennedy, that she pleaded with her mother that they take it home. Former First Lady Jacqueline Kennedy, still clad in black, and grieving the loss of her husband, came to the fair in support of the event, which her husband had initially been behind. Now she had to explain to her daughter that they couldn't take the dog home.

Joe Fowler would declare "There was more of Walt in the Carousel of Progress than in anything else we've done."

Ford Magic Skyway

Initially Walt sought General Motors (GM) to do an exhibit, but they were well underway. Jokingly, they suggested visiting Ford, since GM understood that they had not gotten started off the ground: "They really need you." That proved positive for Disney. Walt and John Hench toured the Dearborn Michigan Ford Plant and was curious about the rollers the cars would go through as they went down the assembly line. Utilizing Ford's technology they created a motion-based system that could host vehicles through the attraction. And not just any vehicles—they were 160 – 1964 convertibles, including the Ford Mustang, which premiered at the Fair.

The original idea was a ride through the USA to points like the Florida everglades, California's redwood forests, and even the Grand Canyon (which Walt had already created at Disneyland in 1958). Ford feared that the tour would be too much akin to GM's slogan "See the USA in Your Chevrolet." They wanted something much bigger.

So bigger it was. Disney brought dinosaurs from the prehistoric realm to the attraction. Caveman eventually appear busy at new developments to include the creating of the wheel. On the backside of this ride through history was a time tunnel to a City of Tomorrow on the move—in Ford cars, of course.

The State of Illinois Presents: Great Moments with Mr. Lincoln

If Walt Disney was the Master Showman, Robert Moses had been the Master Builder. He had led efforts, throughout New York City to revitalize itself—some controversial—and now he was positioned as President of the Fair. Walt was well underway courting corporations when he finally connected one-on-one with Robert Moses. Moses initially thought Walt might create a children's "kiddyland" that could be permanently used after the fair. Walt had bigger ideas in mind. When Robert Moses finally saw a presentation on Abraham

Lincoln, he insisted that the 16th president be at the fair. "I won't open the fair without that exhibit!" Moses labored initially with the U.S. government to no avail to host a larger exhibit that would showcase an entire Hall of Presidents. That didn't happen, but he eventually sold the State of Illinois on the idea of being the host for Great Moments with Mr. Lincoln, even partially reimbursing the state behind the scenes to make it happen.

"Michelangelo and Walt Disney are the stars of my show" acclaimed Robert Moses. His reference to Michelangelo was his success in getting the 465-year-old Pieta masterpiece to be shipped and put on display. The Pieta just had to sit there. Lincoln had to get up and speak several times an hour. While the figure worked seemingly well back in California, the mechanics of the figure or fluctuating electrical currents caused it to be late to open during the initial year of the fair. Still, the response was ecstatic when it was finally figured out. Many didn't believe it was a "robot." Some New Yorkers would toss a coin toward the figure to see if it would flinch.

There was the possibility of another attraction, though the possibility of it came with little more than a year to imagine and build it. But it would be one that would emphasize the New York World's Fair motto, "Peace Through Understanding" better than anyone could have imagined.

Moving Back to California and On to Florida

All these attractions and more found a new home at Disneyland. Great Moments with Mr. Lincoln had a second version that opened up on Main Street USA in 1965 while the original was still playing to audiences in New York. The larger idea of a Hall of Presidents was also in the works but for somewhere else.

For Magic Skyway, the creation of dinosaurs soon found themselves in a Primeval World adjacent to the Grand Canyon Diorama as guests rode the Disneyland Train, and again built for Epcot's Universe of Energy years later. More importantly, the research for the ride system became the basis for a PeopleMover attraction at Disneyland and an omnimover system that would not only move guests all at one time but could take the vehicles and direct them to see what Imagineers wanted them to see. This was used in a Disneyland attraction, Adventure Thru Inner Space, and then infamously, with the Haunted Mansion, built simultaneously for Disneyland and for a new project in Florida.

The highlight of Progressland was transferred to Disneyland in the form of the Carousel of Progress, which, combined with the PeopleMover and the Adventure Thru Inner Space, became the core of an entirely new Tomorrowland at Disneyland in 1967. GE sponsored that attraction and continued a partnership that would continue with Disney for over some 30 years after the fair.

Moreover, they suggested that there was an eager audience in this supposedly more "sophisticated" market that would be open to the magic and charms of Walt Disney. Once Walt remarked to an associate, "Do you realize that we play to only one-fourth of the United States at Disneyland? There's a whole other world on the other side of the Mississippi." As Walt flew back and forth in his Grumman Gulfstream Airplane, he started to make side trips—ones that would lead him to Florida.

Ideas for the Next Century

Consider how you can make the magic come alive for you:

- If Walt Disney was the Master Showman and Robert Moses was the Master Builder, what are you master of? What would you like to be known as master of?

- How can you get others to invest in your ideas?

- How can you bring those investments back home to your organization?

33

"it's a small world"

Finding What Brings Us Together

"A Little Boat Ride"

Three attractions for the New York World's Fair plus attending to the needs of Disneyland was plenty for the staff at WED. (precursors to Walt Disney Imagineering) to labor on. While holding multiple leadership positions throughout Disney at a time when the company was building new attractions like never before, Joe Fowler got a call from Pepsi Corporation about doing an attraction as well for the fair in collaboration with UNICEF (United Nations International Children's Fund). Joe dismissed the offer, saying they didn't have enough time with little more than a year to put it together. This came to the attention of Walt, and it infuriated him. "I'll make those decisions." And he had an idea about how to do it.

So, Walt called together his staff, and began to talk about a "little boat ride" that would celebrate the children of the world in the form of dolls that would sing. In time it would be known as "it's a small world". They would each be dressed in beautiful native costumes in a setting that celebrated each land. He invited artist Mary Blair to come rejoin the organization and to provide a look and style for the attraction. She had come and gone having done work on films like *Cinderella*, *Peter Pan*, and *Alice in Wonderland*. Rolly Crump was working inside Walt Disney Productions as an animator. He had a hobby of making pinwheels. Walt saw it and invited him to work on the project by making a kinetic 120-foot mobile tower in front of the

145

attraction. It would be known as the Tower of the Four Winds. Walt had already begun involving animator Marc Davis on Disneyland projects, and had met Marc's new wife, Alice Davis, one night at a restaurant. Learning that she was a costumer and seamstress, she would come and create the costuming for the dolls. All this, and a little more than a year to do it. Marc would come and provide comic touches to the different scenes. Disney artist Claude Coats, who had a sense of background and layout in doing animation, provided the layout and flow for the entire attraction.

The team not only made it happen in record time, but they repeated the effort when they brought back the attraction to Disneyland. Here they created a bigger façade and entry, and extended the attraction to showcase more countries. The ride would ultimately find a home and wide acclaim in five of the Disney resorts around the world.

One Moon and One Golden Sun

The thread through all of this, and the thing that would make it so much more than just a "little boat ride" would be the music. Initially, the thought was to play the national anthems of each land as passengers rode through the attraction. This created a cacophony of noise. The Sherman Brothers had already achieved success creating hit pop-style songs for former Mouseketeer Annette Funicello, award-winning songs for films like *Mary Poppins*, and music for Disneyland. Walt brought them in to create something for this attraction. The theme of the New York World's Fair was "Peace Through Understanding." Their contribution was a timeless round with the following lyrics:

It's a world of laughter, a world of tears,
It's a world of hope, and a world of fears,
There's so much that we share,
that it's time we're aware,
It's a small world after all.

There is just one moon and one golden sun,
And a smile means friendship to everyone.
Though the mountains are wide,

And the oceans divide
It's a small world after all.

The lyrics for "it's a small world" send a compelling message of harmony and understanding. Yet, the irony of all of this is that the Sherman Brothers, as successful as they were, really didn't enjoy working together. Moreover, they made no association with each other afterwards and their families were practically strangers to one another. Roy Disney referred to their tempers as polar opposites: "Bob is 'Feed the Birds,' Dick is 'Supercalifragilisticexpialidocious.'"

Make no mistake. These were genuine, caring people. At one point, the brothers thought to give the entire royalty of this song to charity. When Walt heard of it, he cautioned the boys against it. "Make a sizeable donation if you would like, but don't donate your royalty to it. This is going to put your children through college." Still, as charitable as they were, there was a gap in their relationship.

It wasn't until 2002, at the London stage premiere of *Chitty Chitty Bang Bang*, that their sons started to reach out to each other. At that time, one brother was living in Beverly Hills and the other in London. As cousins, Gregg and Jeff began to interview people who knew their fathers over the years. Disney legends like Julie Andrews, Roy Disney, Angela Lansbury, and Dick Van Dyke all wanted to share their memories of working with the brothers. When Gregg showed his father the emotional interview done with Kenny Loggins, he turned to his son and agreed to get the families together.

The result became *The Boys: The Sherman Brothers' Story*, a movie that makes no villain out of either brother but simply tries to show how different people work together. While it's ironic that they went so long unable to reconcile personally, it is amazing that what made them come together creatively was their conflict toward each other. That friction created the contribution of an amazing musical library crafted over six decades, far longer than other song-writing greats of that era.

So ironic, from two men who wrote a song we call *it's a small world,* but that they themselves called, *A Prayer for Peace.* The words of the second verse speak of just one moon and one golden sun. In truth, Richard and Robert were the sun and moon to the entire Walt Disney organization. Totally different, but each radiating light in their own way.

Beautiful Clouds of Peace

It's unlikely that Walt and Roy knew much of the Sherman Brothers' differences. But they knew something about the frustrations siblings could share, and many working close with them were caught in the middle. Those moments were sometimes painful, vocal and loud. Walt's long-time secretary Dolores Voght would note of such occasions, "The language was terrible."

As John Hench explained, "Roy's great ambition in life, I suppose, was to stay out of debt. And it was Walt's method in life to keep Roy constantly in debt." In short, Walt wanted money and independence to act on his own, and not be beholden to a board or shareholders. WED became that for him, and by the time the World's Fair came into production, there would be 300 employees reporting up to him.

These and other financial arrangements came to a head and the tension was so palpable that each brother was going through others—particularly Card Walker—to communicate. This was nothing new to the world of "show business" but it was leaving a wedge in the relationship, heightened by threats made by Walt's lawyer.

Eventually tiring of this both brothers agreed to better negotiate. A key turning point was when Roy took the higher road, entered a negotiations meeting and reminded all: "None of us would be here in these offices if it hadn't been for Walt. All your jobs, all the benefits you have, all come from Walt and his contributions." In time a settlement—largely in favor to Walt—was realized. As Roy's birthday approached, Walt sent Roy an Indian peace pipe with a card. "It is wonderful to smoke the Pipe of Peace with you again— the clouds that rise are very beautiful."

Roy put the pipe atop a large portrait of Walt that hung in his office. "We've made peace" he explained to a visitor.

Ideas for the Next Century

Consider how you can make the magic come alive for you:

- How well can you identify others who can contribute and bring their strengths in ways beyond their usual role?

- What do you do to get along better with those you'd rather not work with?

- How well can you separate business from your personal life, preferences, and feelings?

- Do you let the mountains and oceans divide you?

- Are your people one in purpose? Do you cherish what is in common among you? Do you include everyone?

- What clouds of peace need to be made between you and others? How will making that peace make your life better?

34

Project X

Building for the Future

Thinking Much Bigger

In the final years of his life, there were two projects that became the key focus of Walt Disney's efforts. The first was the CalArts project. But the second was to create another physical space for something bigger—bigger than even a theme park. One of Walt's regrets when he built Disneyland was that he simply didn't have enough money for the acreage he sought. Right after the park's initial success, land was bought up left and right and was soon littered with cheap motels, gas stations, fast-food eateries, and retail outlets. The minute you walked or drove off the Disneyland property, you could immediately sense a palpable change from an idyllic setting to total urban chaos.

Walt didn't just want more property—he wanted to address the ills of that urban sprawl. And plenty of it! He not only wanted to see if he could build a theme park, but a resort surrounding it, and then an entire city to complement it. And that required acreage—lots of it. There were discussions of doing park-like projects in other places, from St. Louis, Missouri, to Niagara Falls, New York. But serious land acquisition always turned him further south.

On one trip in particular, they had visited many sites before spending time not only flying over Florida but driving around from Tampa to Ocala. It was on November 22, 1963, that Walt made a choice to seek land out in Central Florida, inland and away from the beaches. Interestingly it was the same area where his father and mother married and first lived in the late 1800s before moving to Chicago. This would be the place to find property.

Returning later that day, the entourage stopped to refuel the aircraft in New Orleans. It's there he learned that President John F. Kennedy had been assassinated. That "just one moon and one golden sun" from his new "it's a small world" attraction seemed needed all the more.

Making a Secret a Reality

As America was caught up in the sorrows of a lost president and in the hopes of a World's Fair, Walt Disney organized a very tight team of individuals who would go about purchasing contiguous properties in the Orlando area under a variety of pseudonyms. These "dummy" corporations included names like Reedy Creek Ranch Corporation, Latin-American Development, and M.T. Lott. The initial purchase would come to about twice the size of the City of Manhattan—and at an average of $185 an acre!

By the time the Fair in New York had concluded in the fall, the property was largely purchased, and key players of their own were looking for a place to hold a press conference for Disney in Orlando, Florida. It's difficult to determine exactly how Emily Bavar, a reporter from the *Orlando Sentinel-Star* came to know about the plan. A key community influencer may have given her boss some insight. When a larger group of Disney executives were told about the project in June of 1965, they may have individually sought out properties of their own, but didn't conceal their identities as well.

It certainly seemed like Disney was giving Emily a window of opportunity when she and other press agents were invited to attend a series of promotional events tied to the 10th anniversary of Disneyland. There in a group interview, she asked Walt about whether Disney was acquiring land in the Orlando area. In her words, "He looked like I had thrown a bucket of water in his face." He, of course, denied such was the case, but then gave her an upper hand by detailing all of the reasons as to why it wouldn't work given climate, population numbers, and tourism figures. Then she asked if the New York Fair shows were all moving to Disneyland, California.

"Of course," was his quick reply, "there is only one Disneyland." Then almost but not quite as an afterthought he added, "as such."

Shortly thereafter, on October 24th, Bavar published an article in the *Sentinel-Star:*

"WE SAY: 'MYSTERY' INDUSTRY IS DISNEY."

Governor W. Haydon Burns was allowed to make the official announcement, on October 25th in Miami to the Florida League of Municipalities Convention, that Walt Disney Productions was the "mystery industry" coming to Central Florida and that it "will build the greatest attraction yet known in the history of Florida." The audience erupted with "wild applause."

On November 15, 1956, Walt, Roy, and Governor Burns hosted a conference at the Cherry Plaza Hotel in Orlando. Here Walt announced plans for a Disneyland-style park and resort. But he also hinted at something much, much more.

Back in California, an office available to only a few had been set up to build out what would go into Project X. Only this time, the project would have five letters not one—E.P.C.O.T.—Experimental Prototype Community of Tomorrow. In time it would be displayed as EPCOT, EPCOT Center, and then simply, Epcot. But written in any form, it was to be some sort of blueprint and showpiece for the future.

Walt saw a "Great Big Beautiful Tomorrow." And he bought a great big, beautiful property to create it.

Now if only he could live on to see it.

Ideas for the Next Century

Consider how you can make the magic come alive for you:

- What is your "Project X"?

- How big are your ideas? Do you have enough room for them?

- Who do you bring into your inner circle to make your ideas come alive?

- What do you keep confidential? What do you share with others? Why?

35

The End of an American Original

What is Your Legacy?

Not Enough Time

Time was hastening on. There were so many projects on Walt's docket.

Films like *Blackbeard's Ghost* were filming at the studio, *The Happiest Millionaire* was in editing, and *Follow Me, Boys!* would be released December 1, 1966. Animated film projects included *The Jungle Book*, slated for 1967, and an animated featurette (longer than a short, shorter than a full-length animated film) called *Winnie the Pooh and the Honey Tree*.

Television included the anthology series, *Walt Disney's Wonderful World of Color*, and included Walt Disney hosting the beginning of each show.

In 1960, Walt personally invested in the Celebrity Sports Center in Denver, Colorado, along with other celebrities. Two years later, Walt Disney Productions bought out all interests and ran it exclusively. It became a training ground in recreation management for the company.

After hosting the ceremonies for the Winter Olympics in Squaw Valley, Walt saw the potential of a winter-style resort. The company struck a deal with the US Forest Service to develop a project known as Mineral King.

CalArts was in model form and under development. Land had been identified and construction was soon to occur.

At Disneyland, Walt had created a new land in the form of New Orleans Square and had dedicated it in 1966. Here he would sandwich the land with a Pirates of the Caribbean and a sort of Haunted Mansion. A brand-new Tomorrowland would follow that. All those projects were in development and under construction.

And the Florida Project? His team was locked in a conference room drafting plans, while others were flying to and from Central Florida making sense of this exceptionally large swampland.

But having all of this on his plate was not Walt's problem. It was his health. He couldn't do what he used to, and he had to make priorities. Ron Miller, his son-in-law, explained Walt's reaction.

> The doctor said, "Walt, you're not going to be able to work fourteen hours a day like you've been doing." I think right then and there Walt thought, "Well, what is most important to work on? Disney World!" He realized that Disney World and EPCOT were not something he could build in just a year or two.

So, he focused on the Florida Project. To get government and the public on board, Walt insisted on filming a short presentation that would sell people on this idea of EPCOT . Marty Sklar penned the script and Walt got in front of the cameras selling the idea of what the Florida project would look like. Yes, there would be a Disneyland-style park, but the center of this would be the city of the future. This presentation outlined the possibilities of such a venture—bigger than anything Walt had taken on before.

Ron Miller noted: "When Walt was ill, he said, "If I could live for fifteen more years, I would surpass everything I've done over the last forty years."

Running Out of Time

Walt's health greatly deteriorated during this time. He had long had a dry, nagging cough, but it had worsened. Moreover, it simply took a toll on him. A lifetime of cigarette smoking, common among so many of that era, finally asserted its consequences.

But it was neck and back pain, believed to have come from earlier years of polo, that caused Walt to go into surgery on his spine. It was there, X-rays detected a tumor, and that necessitated the removal of most of his left lung, Unfortunately, by the time it had been found and removed, the cancer had spread to other parts of his body.

There were 4,000 people working for Walt Disney Productions at that time. Those close to him saw the effects of the cobalt treatment he had on his weakening condition. People who saw him in the final days saw a fragile man. But many of the same couldn't fathom a day without Walt. Looking back later, they realized they saw the signs but didn't put them together. One such situation was when Marc Davis showed Walt several sketches he had made for a bear band that would appear at the ski resort project at Mineral King (it would later be created for the Magic Kingdom at Walt Disney World). As Walt left, he turned to Davis and said, "Goodbye Marc." He had never heard Walt say goodbye before. It was indicative of several intimate and tender moments those close to him had during those last days.

Upon returning from the premiere of *Follow Me, Boys!* in New York, Walt's brother Roy visited him across the street at the hospital. Walt lay there using tiles on the ceiling to map out how he saw EPCOT mapped out. In what would be his final visit with Lillian, he held her tight and strong. She thought he would make it, as did Roy.

But Walt didn't make it. On December 15, 1966, in St. Joseph's Hospital, across from Walt Disney Productions in Burbank, Walt passed away at age 65 of "an acute circulatory collapse." There was no mention of cancer.

What Was Walt Disney's Legacy?

The organization would reel from the loss of its leader. The experience created deep reflection for decades after about Walt Disney, and why he so stood out.

The *New York Times* asserted :

> Starting from very little—save a talent for drawing, a gift of imagination that was somehow in tune with everyone's imagination, and a dogged determination to succeed—Walt Disney became one of Hollywood's master entrepreneurs and one of the world's greatest entertainers. He had a genius for innovation, his production was enormous, he was able to keep sure and personal control over his increasingly far-flung enterprise, and his hand was ever on the public pulse. He was, in short, a legend in his own lifetime—and so honored many times over. Yet none of this sums up Walt Disney....

Eric Sevareid's summary on the CBS Evening News Affirmed: "He was an original. Not just an American original, but an original."

Truly the world saw him very much as a Master Showman, as an extraordinary entrepreneur, even as an original. But what did those closest to him think? From *Remembering Walt: Favorite Memories of Walt Disney*, we read the following:

Former Mouseketeer Sharon Baird reminisced:

> Walt Disney wanted the Mouseketeers to call him Uncle Walt. We respected him so much though, we couldn't call him Uncle Walt. We called him Mr. Disney. But if he were here today, I would call him Uncle, *Uncle* Walt to make up for all the years I didn't call him "Uncle Walt." Now that I'm older, I understand what it would have meant to him to have us call him Uncle Walt.

By the time Walt had passed on, Hayley Mills had gone from a small girl to a major movie star, having been in 7 Disney films to include *Pollyanna* and *The Parent Trap*. She observed the following:

> A lot of Walt's personal philosophy has rubbed off on me. He was absolutely right, you have to focus on the good things. I think he really did love people. Only the cynics say, "He was onto a good thing and saw he could make a lot of money." Walt believed in what he was doing. He believed in being a positive force for good. He believed in people and that was why he was successful.

Dick Nunis recalled:

> The most valuable thing I learned from Walt was the importance of people. I've learned that the higher you go in an organization, the less you do, the more you worry, and the more you depend on people. I think Walt depended on people a great deal, probably more than they realize. He had the intuitive ability to be as nice to a person busing the tables as to the president of a company and everybody in between.

Finally, Richard Sherman experienced Walt along with his brother:

> Walt had a great love for the Song "Feed the Birds." The image came out of the book *Mary Poppins*; we used it as a symbol of kindness. Many times, late on Fridays, he'd call us into his office and say, "What have you been working on?" We'd chat for a while and then he'd say, "Dick, play that song for me." As I played and sang "Feed the Birds," he'd gaze out the window, get misty-eyed and say, "That's what it's all about, isn't it?"

This is but a sample of what those who worked with him shared. As noted earlier, they are the same people Walt's daughter, Diane Disney, speaks of when she stated: "Thirty years after his death, a number of former employees still welled up with tears when they talked about his passing." It was more than the box office success or the new park attractions. Optimism, ideals, philosophies, and

158

relationships are at the heart of Walt Disney's legacy. This is why he was an American original.

Ideas for the Next Century

Consider how you can make the magic come alive for you:

- What are all the projects you have on your plate?

- Of those projects, what matters most?

- What projects would you focus on if you were running out of time?

- *Who* would you focus on if you were running out of time?

- What legacy would you want to leave for others if you were to run out of time?

36

What Would Walt Do?

What Traditions Define You?

When a Star Stands Still

While it looks like winter on Matterhorn Mountain year-round, there's no time of the year more beautiful than the holiday season at Disneyland. For years, special holiday decorations and a parade have graced Disneyland, and, at one time, a large star stood at the top of the Matterhorn. It even lit up and rotated.

Unfortunately for Disney Cast Members, the month of December 1966 was not a happy time. Those working at Disneyland were in shock, even after the band surrounded the flag retreat and softly played, "When You Wish Upon a Star."

In that state of shock, several managers, including Van France, sought refuge at a lounge located at the Disneyland Hotel. There, they shared remembrances for several hours.

Van recalls the experience in his own work, *Windows on Main Street*. As they got ready to leave, one member of management turned to the other and mentioned that the star on top of the Matterhorn had broken again. The other manager shrugged it off, as if to say, "Why bother?" At that moment, his colleague turned to him and said, "You wouldn't shrug it off if Walt were here."

A few years later, the star was removed but the conversation marked the beginning of a dialogue that has continued to this day, with Cast Members asking, "What would Walt do?" That philosophy carried the organization forward for many years. In part, it worked because Walt had laid down key principles about how to run the park. Partly out of loyalty, and partly out of habit, Cast Members referred to those ideals.

Defining the Tradition

Dick Nunis shares another story involving Van France that same very difficult day. Dick was driving into work when he heard on the radio that Walt had died. He called Card Walker and asked whether Disneyland should open. Card didn't know but called a few minutes later and said to open the park. Dick pushed back about how upset the employees might be. Card responded, "Lilly made this decision and I'll tell you what she said, 'Walt would say the show must go on.'"

Dick got the park opened, though he would be criticized by the press. Then he got with Van France and said, "Van, we've got to start worrying about the next training book. That's when we came up with the idea of *The Traditions* concept so that Walt's words, traditions and philosophies would go on forever. We had a rough format by the end of the day. So on the day Walt died, the show did go on."

That *Traditions* carries on today. It is the title of the orientation program all Disney Cast Members go through. It speaks of Disney's heritage, service vision, its values, and the behaviors expected of everyone. But what is the *tradition* of Walt Disney?

As one of Walt's most tenured animators, Ward Kimball, remarked that if you were instinctively in tune, you wouldn't have to ask the question, What would Walt do? He himself had learned excellence intuitively. Ward learned that excellence, as Walt had taught, was not in repeating one's self, or in going back in time to consider what others would do, but in moving forward and in bringing new ideas to the table. After all, he reasoned, that is just exactly what Walt would have done.

That is the *Disney Tradition*.

Roy Disney Steps into His Brother's Shoes

No one at Walt Disney Productions was more affected by Walt's death than his brother Roy. Studio writer Jack Speirs shared:

> After Walt had died, I went out one evening to get my car. And along came Walt's brother Roy. He was walking slow. He stepped out on the curb and stopped. He just stood there and took a long look around the Studio. He slowly looked the whole place over. Together, he and Walt had built all of this—and now Walt was gone—just gone. Roy dropped his head, looked at the ground, walked across the lot, got in his car, and drove away. It was one of the saddest things I have ever seen.

At age 73, Roy was planning to retire at the time of Walt's death. He never saw himself as outliving his brother. But now Walt was gone. Someone needed to step in. That retirement would be postponed— indefinitely.

Roy made the following statement:

> As President and Chairman of the Board of Walt Disney Productions I want to assure the public, our stockholders, and each of our more than 4000 employees that we will continue to operate Walt Disney's company in the way he has established and guided it. Walt Disney spent his entire life and almost every waking hour in the creative planning of motion pictures, Disneyland, television shows, and all the other diversified activities that have carried his name through the years. Around him Walt Disney gathered the kind of creative people who understood his way of communicating with the public through entertainment. Walt's ways were

always unique, and he built a unique organization. A team of creative people that he was justifiably proud of.

About a week after Walt's death, Roy gathered the key executives of the organization, including Card Walker and Donn Tatum. Gathering these leaders together he assumed the mantle and confirmed that Walt Disney Productions would go forward in the same manner that Walt had outlined. Specifically, Roy spoke of the Florida project declaring "We're going to finish this park, and we're going to do it just the way Walt wanted it Don't you ever forget it. I want every one of you to do just exactly what you were going to do when Walt was alive."

In an interview with Bob Thomas, who would later pen Roy's official biography as well as Walt's, Bob asked Roy about Walt:

> Success changes everyone, especially in Hollywood, where success is exaggerated. With Walt, I think success made him drive harder. He was always saying, in effect, "You ain't seen nothin' yet." If he had a big success, he was eager to go on to the next one. For that reason, he would never make sequels.

The American Original would never have a sequel. But he would have his brother Roy.

Ideas for the Next Century

Consider how you can make the magic come alive for you:

- What are the traditions you have that define who you are?

- What traditions do you have that define excellence?

- If you had to take over for someone else, how would you move forward?

- What does success do to you? How do you respond to it?

37

Pirates of the Caribbean

Building the Standard
for All Others

Setting Sail to a New Kind of Attraction

At the time of Walt's passing, a new attraction was being installed at
Disneyland. Arguably by many the greatest attraction ever built, it at
least may well be one of the most favored attractions of all time. It is
to Disney parks what *Mary Poppins*, as was spoken earlier, was to the
studios at Walt Disney Productions. Bob Gurr observed in *The
Imagineering Story*, that Pirates was "the high point of how you design
and operate an attraction...the way to tell stories in the most
thorough manner."

By the end of the first 5 years of operating Disneyland, it became
apparent to Walt what kinds of attractions were appealing most to
guests. Part of that had to do with ambitious projects like creating a
bobsled style coaster inside a scaled replica of Matterhorn Mountain,
or an underwater journey via a submarine voyage, or a highway-in-
the-sky vehicle like the monorail. But Walt knew that plussing up
existing attractions was important, and so he invited Marc Davis
after working on unforgettable villains like Maleficent and Cruella de
Ville to go down to Disneyland and make his observations and
critiques of the attractions. Marc felt the Jungle Cruise and the Mine

Train Through Nature's Wonderland failed to carry any sense of warmth or humor, and was in fact, boring.

One of the first steps toward improvement was bringing in animation talent like Marc to help with not only taking existing attractions to a better level, but also creating new attractions that would have greater sense of artistry. Not that Walt hadn't already brought former artists over to Imagineering. But he wanted to bring fresh, new blood—and ideas—into the thinking.

All Hands on Deck

Walt invited Marc Davis to "plus" the attractions and then he gave him the opportunity of working on the idea of a Pirate Wax Museum. But it wouldn't stay as a walking tour for very long. Claude Coats, also a former animator but also a layout and background artist, Was brought in to create entire themed spaces. He ensured that the concept was built out in such a way that not only a greater, more immersive space could be built, but that it could accommodate more people. Having learned from the use of boats in the New York World's Fair attraction, "it's a small world," Walt clearly saw this was a better vehicle for addressing capacity than a walk-through experience. Claude encompassed the ride technology with another far distant world in space and time.

That same attention to using the talent and skills of the organization to create something fantastic materialized as Walt brought others onboard like Blaine Gibson, a sculptor. Gibson crafted the 16th President for Great Moments with Mr. Lincoln. He now sculpted a scallywag crew to include men, women, goats, dogs, chickens, and more.

Yale Gracey took on special effects, creating a fire sequence so real that the Anaheim Fire Department requested switches on the sprinkler system so that in the case of a fire, the effects could be cut off so fire workers could find the *actual* flames.

The dialogue and narrative for the attraction was written by Imagineer Xavier "X" Atencio, another recruit from the Animation team. This attraction had so many details, even in the script. For that reason, Xavier Atencio was concerned about Guests understanding everything people were saying in the script he wrote. Walt replied, "Don't worry about it. It's like a cocktail party. People come to cocktail parties, and they tune in a conversation over here, then a conversation over there. Each time the guest comes through here, they'll hear something else. That'll bring them back time and again." Walt, knowing the strengths of his team, invited Atencio to create the theme song, "Yo Ho, Yo Ho, a Pirate's Life for Me". Yet Atencio had never written a song before.

The Ship's Real Captain

Walt Disney passed away three months before Pirates of the Caribbean opened. If he had lived longer, he would have seen that the attraction became one of the most popular Disney attractions of all time. But who would have imagined the power in that brand, even to the point of reinventing the pirate movie genre.

Ultimately, who led all of this? Sculptor Blaine Gibson gives the credit for that to Walt Disney. "It boils down to just one man—Walt. It just verifies how right he was. We were all just going along for the ride."

It's fitting that Pirates would be the last attraction Walt would spend the greatest attention on, and the first to premiere after his departure. It combines all that he knew in creating a great theme park experience and uses his best talents in making it so. It is also amazing that it would be the basis for a hallmark cinematic venture years later. Marty Sklar said, "Pirates is Disney's quintessential, signature attraction...We measure everything we do against Pirates of the Caribbean."

Ideas for the Next Century

Consider how you can make the magic come alive for you:

- How do you take everything you know and put it together to create the best product or experience possible—one that people can't get enough of?

- How do you bring "all hands on deck" to make a concept a reality?

- Is there something you have done that is the yardstick for everything else you do? What makes it define your standard?

38

Nine Old Men

Building Strong Teams

Walt was once asked what happens after Disney. In a 1963 National Geographic interview he said, "I think about that. Every day I'm throwing more responsibility to other men. Every day I'm trying to organize them more strongly."

Establishing the Nine Old Men

In the aftermath of the strike, Walt sought to organize an Animation Board in 1940 that would address animation issues and the management of the animators themselves. This evolved over time, but by the 1950's it became known as Walt's Nine Old Men. Nine Old Men was a reference to President Franklin D. Roosevelt's members of the Supreme Court. They stood in opposition to many of Roosevelt's efforts during the Depression. The difference here was that Walt's Nine Old Men were fairly young, leading the pack, and were some of the most faithful to Walt.

The Nine Old Men included Frank Thomas, Ollie Johnston, John Lounsbery, Marc Davis, Ward Kimball, Woolie Reitherman, Les Clark, Eric Larson, and Milt Kahl. Together, they held animation together for some twenty-five years, constantly working to improve the craft and cement Disney's legacy as *the* leader in animation.

Others over the years tried to compete with Disney, some with success here and there, but as Paul Terry, who created Terrytoons with characters like Mighty Mouse, pointed out: "Walt Disney is the Tiffany's of this business, and we're the Woolworth's." These artists were the craftsmen who made Disney the "Tiffany's" of the animation industry.

A New Swinging Chapter

With Disneyland in the 1950's taking so much of his time, animators were soon galvanizing around the leadership of the Nine Old Men to accomplish the work needed. Many others offered important support to others, but these individuals either helped lead the animators or animated projects themselves. Over time, this led to mixed results. *Sleeping Beauty* was a masterpiece—a painting that came to life due to the artistic influence of Eyvind Earle. But it took too long, cost too much money, and, in the short term, provided too little return to the studio.

To save costs moving forward, *One Hundred and One Dalmatians* employed new technologies developed by Ub Iwerks allowing xerography (an early copy machine) to copy the drawings onto cells, reducing time and money. Beyond critical acclaim, the box office returns were significant and supported Walt Disney Productions in being able to pay off a 22-year-old liability to the Bank of America.

And yet, Walt hated the visual style of the film, and he seemed ready to drop animation altogether. Add to that his continuous focus not only on Disneyland but the New York World's Fair and the purchase of land in Florida—these projects robbed him of any time to pay attention to the next film, *Sword in the Stone*, released in 1963. It was budgeted at 40 percent less than *One Hundred and One Dalmatians*. It too suffered from Walt's lack of interest, as Milt Kahl put it: "He was interested in a picture until he had all the problems solved and then he lost interest."

Realizing this was not working and in an effort to keep the animation studio from any further decline, Walt took a more personal investment in animating Rudyard Kipling's classic, *The Jungle Book*.

But his first instruction to the core team working on it, was to not read the book. Walt had something else in mind for it—or someone else in mind. Phil Harris was attending the same event as Walt in Palm Springs, and immediately Walt could see him in the role of Baloo, who in time became as big—if not bigger—than the boy Mowgli himself. Along with other characters in the film, the tone moved from one of being a dark setting in the jungle to being the coolest, swingingest beat of the 1960s. Even the vultures (Buzzy, Dizzy, Flaps, and Ziggy) were intended to be a play on The Beatles— though the band members turned them down on voicing the roles themselves.

Walt spent as much time as he could on the film. Indeed, the film is more about Walt the Showman than it is about Kipling, and his writings. But Walt died in December 1966, before the film premiered, and it really was many of the Nine Old Men who led it across the finish line by October of 1967. The film was a box office sensation earning more money than any previous animation film during its initial run.

The Formula Becomes Formulaic

The Jungle Book was a lifesaver, for in the absence of Walt's protection, Roy initially discussed in close circles that perhaps animation should fold. The time and cost were considerable, and after all, how many animated features could you create?

Walt's Nine Old Men held the role of protecting the heart and soul of Walt Disney Productions at this time. But many of the Nine Old Men were now—well—old. By this time Marc Davis had become fully involved with Imagineering. Ward Kimball had taken on several live-action and television projects before retiring in the mid-seventies, along with Les Clark, the oldest of the team who had originally learned the trade from Ub Iwerks back in 1927.

New blood was needed, and Eric Larson created a training program to help generate that, but how do you add new blood if you don't see a future for this industry?

It was clearly a time of uncertainty, and with fewer animators than before, economics-of-scale took place with the next two features, *The Aristocats* and *Robin Hood*. These were both directed by Woolie Reitherman, one of the Nine Old Men, who had also directed *Sword in the Stone*, *One Hundred and One Dalmatians*, and *The Jungle Book*.

These films began to follow certain redundant and recycled patterns to include the following:

Story Lines: Both *One Hundred and One Dalmatians* and *The Aristocats* were about pets who had to find their way home.

Tone: *Jungle Book* and *The Aristocats* took on a Sixties aesthetic in narrative, music, and approach.

Voice Characters: Watch the films and you keep hearing the same voices in your head. Actors like Pat Buttram can be heard in *The Aristocats* (Napoleon) and *Robin Hood* (Sheriff of Nottingham). George Lindsey played in *Aristocats* (Lafayette) and *Robin Hood* (Trigger). Worst of all, Phil Harris is in *Jungle Book* (Baloo), *The Aristocats* (Thomas O'Malley), and *Robin Hood* (Little John).

Animation: To save time and money, films like *The Aristocats* and *Robin Hood* copied line drawn animation from previous animated films. For instance, the dance scene in *Robin Hood* is parallel to the dance sequence in *Snow White and the Seven Dwarfs*. Getting small pets on the back of a truck was repeated in both *One Hundred and One Dalmatians* as well as *The Aristocats*—only the truck is pointed differently.

All these films did well for themselves and for that era, though none as well as *Jungle Book*. While played out in different locales or settings, these films ultimately felt clichéd and somewhat out-of-place as the years distanced themselves from Walt's presence. It felt very much like the same "What would Walt do?" played out again and again. In particular, newer artists ready to do something fresh and interesting, felt they couldn't fight the formula in place.

Tim Burton of *Nightmare Before Christmas* acclaim, who was first hired at the studio several years after *Robin Hood's* production, would describe it as a place still run by lost men, unsure how to move forward. And the Nine Old Men were not only becoming old, so was their art form. It survived this period, but changing times were ahead.

Catching the Bug Under the Briny Sea

Meanwhile, Disney live-action theatrical releases in the years following Walt were on a roller coaster. Riding the wave of all things *Mary Poppins*, the studio sought to find another major musical success with *Bedknobs and Broomsticks*. Intended to star Julie Andrews, Angela Lansbury ended up with the starring role, alongside David Tomlinson. With music from the Sherman brothers and animated sequences like *Mary Poppins*, its formula should have been successful. But in the wake of the *Sound of Music* by 20th Century Fox, no musical would ever rival what Julie Andrews had brought twice to the screen.

However, one unique exception at the box office was *The Love Bug*, which out of the blue made almost as much money as *Jungle Book*. It was the second top grossing film of 1969, just behind *Butch Cassidy and the Sundance Kid*, and well ahead of the expensively made *Hello, Dolly* by 20th Century Fox. The film starred Dean Jones, Buddy Hackett and even David Tomlinson, but audiences were most drawn toward a Volkswagen that came alive.

Ideas for the Next Century

Consider how you can make the magic come alive for you:

- When do you get in and support your team? When do you let them move forward on their own?

- When does your formula for success become formulaic?

- How do you bring others on board to help pave a future forward?

39

The Haunted Mansion

The Spirit of Compromise

Creatives Need to Compromise

The Haunted Mansion had long been considered for Disneyland. It originally began as more of a decrepit, haunted house off of Main Street. Even the mansion building was in place for years before it opened its gates to the public. But what it would ultimately become was left to Imagineers at WED after Walt's passing. Indeed, this was probably the first significant attraction to really be completed without complete direction.

Walt asserted that "Everything here at Disneyland and at the Studio is a team effort." That was especially difficult since the Studio was made up of artists with individual talents. Putting them together was not always easy. A defining point came after Walt passed away, while the organization was in the middle of creating the infamous Haunted Mansion.

Anyone who studies the Disney organization in depth will find that the miracle of Disney animation is that it took so many creative, disparate artists and put them together to create a cohesive whole— one that no one gets to put their name on, except for Disney. The same could be said of the Imagineers that made up WED. Responsible for creating attractions, the requirement sought to bring in not only a wider range of creative expertise from all sorts of backgrounds such as character development, prop production, special FX, and interior design, but also combine that right-brained talent with the left-brain sensibility of engineers, draftsmen, and mechanics who have to make these buildings stand up and the attractions therein run day in and day out.

Kim Irvine, as a child visiting the Model Shop where her mother worked, could see that in action. It was Yale Gracey who, as an "Illusioneer," sought to create a delivered séance in a crystal ball. In trying out a new effect in the attraction, Kim's mother stood in as the model for the face of Madame Leota. At the hands of sculptor Blaine Gibson, a sort of "death mask was made of her mother, ironically named Leota "Lee" Toombs Thomas. And it was animation legend Ub Iwerks and his son Don, who employed projection technology to bring Madame Leota to life. Of this, Kim Irvine remarked "They had a camaraderie that was just incredible. I always hoped that I was going to be a part of it as well."

Still, teamwork involves compromise—and that's a word to which many who have strong artistic or creative sensibilities don't like to yield. Compromise in the eyes of many symbolizes "giving up" something really great for something much lesser. It can be thought of as a "watering down" of great ideas.

In times past, conflicts would be settled by Walt. Now it was Roy who was in charge, and he took no ownership in the idea that he was a creative decision maker. But both he and Walt did understand the importance of working together as brothers—even though at times they had major fallouts with each other. Roy knew that moving the organization forward required the same of everyone at Walt Disney Productions. Once, when two department heads quarreled, Roy sent a telegram on December 29, 1942, by overnight wire—declaring, "I don't see why you two can't work together. You are both working for the same company...none of us should have any pride of authorship of ideas but give and take and work with each other amicably. Happy New Year." That sense of teamwork was at the core of the Disney culture—especially now that Walt was gone.

Scarcity Offers Opportunities for Creative Compromise

Where conflict and compromise often occurred was in the limits of what one could do creatively. To understand this, Imagineer Marty Sklar would often talk about two views of a blank sheet of paper:

> There are two ways to look at a blank sheet of paper. It can be the most frightening thing in the world because you have to make the first mark on it. Or it can be the greatest opportunity in the world, because you get to make the first mark—you can let your imagination fly in any direction and create whole new worlds!

All of this is true, but additionally, there is another element to this. Even a blank sheet of paper with all of its possibilities has limitations. You can't do anything outside the four boundaries of that sheet of paper. So it is with designing attractions. Even Imagineers don't usually have unlimited budgets. Requisites like centering on a particular intellectual property or fitting inside a specific physical space, or worse, having it done by yesterday, all are boundaries to that blank sheet of paper. And for creative artists or brilliant engineers—those things can be frustrating. People like this often push back on limitations being made of them. In one Imagineering book the question is asked, "How many Imagineers does it take to change a lightbulb?" The answer? "Does it have to be a lightbulb?"

With such limits, creative compromise is crucial. There are instances of this that play out in the Haunted Mansion. For example, there is little space in the actual mansion home built in New Orleans Square. Certainly not enough to put an entire ride through it. And railroad tracks are just behind the building. In essence, to "go off-the-page" a stretch room was brainstormed (two, actually, for efficiency's sake). The stretch room was really intended to create a way for guests to be lowered by a large elevator down to a basement level so they could walk through to the other side of the railroad berm, and then board a ride vehicle that takes them through a warehouse out behind.

176

Marc Davis conceived the stretching portraits. For the stretch room, Claude Coats sought to counter the amusement of the portraits with a certain foreboding—one in the form of lightning, and a hanging corpse. As noted in *The Imagineering Story*, "That duality was in part a reflection of the dynamic between Imagineers Davis and Coats. Davis's drawings leaned toward the amusing, while Coats's creations were more intensely scary. From the start, this combination set the tone for the rest of the attraction—creepiness with wit, spookiness with a wink."

Other Imagineers brought their experience and creativity to bear. Yale Gracey perfected the "Peppers Ghost" effect made popular decades prior in vaudeville acts. It allows the ghosts to appear and disappear in places like the Ballroom. The effect is made possible by installing during construction large and long panes of glass between the Guests and the ballroom. There the images would be projected on the glass, but Guests would never see the panes.

That is, until someone took a gun in 1974 and shot a bullet through one of the panes of glass. It didn't shatter the pane, but it did result in a bullet hole right through—destroying the effect. Imagineers struggled with how to address this, as removing the pane of glass, and replacing it would require opening up the ceiling of the building and reinstalling a new pane—a solution costly in time, labor, and money. A brilliant "off-the-page" solution was to place a small spider and web over the hole. The solution fixed the problem at a fraction of the price.

Providing Great Opportunities to Create

One of Walt's key approaches to bringing exceptional people together to work on something involved: Providing opportunities to do new things and push new boundaries. Walt's paradigm on this was:

> There's really no secret about our approach—opening new doors and doing new things—because we're curious. And curiosity keeps leading us down new paths. We're always

177

exploring and experimenting...we call it Imagineering—the blending of creative imagination and technical know-how.

But make no mistake, even when Walt asked someone to not worry so much about even the budget, there were still boundaries—even if there were new ones. Those boundaries became seemingly more defined in the absence of Walt Disney.

For instance, Rolly Crump was tasked at one point to add to what would be the Haunted Mansion. His take was in essence, weird. And when Walt first saw it late one afternoon, he couldn't even make sense of it. Rolly thought that his approach was "dead" until 7:30 the next morning. As Rolly walked into his office, he found Walt sitting in his chair, wearing the same clothes from the day before. "You son of a bitch," Walt said, "I couldn't sleep last night...[from] all that weird stuff you showed me yesterday." Walt encouraged Rolly to press forward, identifying objects, props, and furnishings that might be collected as if it were a "museum of the weird."

At one point, Rolly shared, "I put my hand on [Walt's] arm and said, 'Did I go too far?' Walt retorted, 'No...You go as far as you want...I'm the one to bring you back if it's necessary.' The conversation continued until finally Walt got up and went home to bed."

There are many pieces related to Rolly's "weird" creativity in the Haunted Mansion, but it was never what Rolly had hoped it would become. After Walt's death, Dick Irvine sent Rolly to work on other projects at Disneyland.

By then, several other artists had taken turns creating some kind of spooky, alley-style experience. In time, there formed two frames of thought on the Mansion. One group of Imagineers, led by Claude Coats, provided a sort of moody, dark experience. The other group, largely led by Marc Davis, took from his success with Pirates of the Caribbean and the redo on the Jungle Cruise to create a montage of funny experiences. Both groups went back and forth. It came down to scary vs. silly. In the past, Walt would typically break such ties. Now they had to work it out alone.

178

Leslie Iwerks, granddaughter and author of The Imagineering Story, wrote of Davis and Coats during the creation of Pirates of the Caribbean: "Davis's partnership with Coats was something of an odd-couple pairing, since Coats was quiet and introspective and Davis was outgoing and assertive, but it generated a dynamic blend of immersive detailed sets with a lively, expressive cast of Audio-Animatronic actors."

Tony Baxter, in Jason Surrell's *Haunted Mansion* book, explains that the compromise ended up creating a sort of three-act play—one that enacted the creepiness of Claude Coats in the first third, the comedy of the Davis graveyard scenes in the third part, and a marriage of the two during the ballroom and attic scenes. And all of that sprinkled with a weird little bit of Rolly Crump throughout.

A Compromised Reception

When the Haunted Mansion finally opened at Disneyland, everyone lined up. Anticipation was huge. Enormous crowds queued on that side of the park between the still-new Pirates of the Caribbean and Haunted Mansion. Yet guest reviews were somewhat mixed. Many baby boomers were in their teenage years and were looking for something much scarier. In time, the attraction became known not so much for its fear factor, but for its attention to so much haunting detail. It is timeless because of its mix of creepy and funny.

Still, the compromise paid off, because while there was still a moment or two of shriek, there were plenty of details to catch. Along with Pirates, Jungle Cruise, and "it's a small world", these rides became the signature attractions that are synonymous with Disneyland and the other Magic Kingdom-style parks—something that guests want to re-ride again and again.

Perhaps that's why every major attraction at Disney goes through years of development before it opens to the public. From initial idea to opening day, there is a long process in creating a great Guest experience. But few attractions have had a longer development period than the Haunted Mansion, which opened to Guests in October 1969. As mentioned earlier, even before Disneyland opened in 1955, there were ideas relating to the old, weathered home at the end of one of the side streets off Main Street, USA at Disneyland. But it took many tries and many teams of individuals to fashion it into the mansion we know today.

In the end, the creative compromises that were made on the attraction not only served to make it a better Guest experience, but it has made the attraction both timeless and popular. Sometimes you have to use a little creative compromise. It can be interesting to see where other great ideas can be married to yours if you are open to creative compromise.

Ideas for the Next Century

Consider how you can make the magic come alive for you:

- How do you reach consensus or compromise as a team?

- How can you avoid the obsession of always being right in your view and others being wrong in theirs?

- How can you spend more time thinking about how to bring everyone's ideas to the table rather than making sure your own idea wins out?

- Where do you allow people to work past the borders of the page into ideas that could never be held on a page?

- How can you build trust not only in each other, but in the concept that the best ideas can prevail if you let them simmer to the top?

A World on the Move

Taking the High Road Toward Excellence

In 1967, a new Tomorrowland was built for Disneyland. It would often be referred to as "a World on the Move." But the biggest Tomorrowland being built was across the country. And this world— Walt Disney World—was indeed a world not just on the move, but one taking the high road toward excellence.

There were many events that shaped the building of Walt Disney World. Key moments included the following happenings.

A Government-Approved "Carrot"

While Roy declared that the Florida project would move forward, it seemed to many that there was little progress made in the year following Walt's death. Part of this was because the necessary government infrastructure had to be approved and put in place. Bob Foster, who was at the center of the land purchases, and who helped create for that infrastructure acknowledged : "Without a municipality, Walt Disney World would never have been built... We would have had multilayers of governmental influence, building permits, inspections, zoning matters, both local and state."

To that end, Roy proposed creating a structure, entitled the Reedy Creek Improvement District (RCID), for handling those issues. Roy wasn't certain at the time that it would be sanctioned. He also knew that if he simply turned around and sold the acreage purchased in Florida, he would stand to make enormous sums of money. But RCID was an absolute if Walt Disney World was to be built. To get the legislature on board, they showed the EPCOT film Walt had created just months prior.

When Walt and Roy met with officials earlier, Walt insisted that there would only ever be one Disneyland, but in his mind, there could be a much better Disney World—one with not just a theme park, but a city of the future as well. Rather than the castle being the "carrot" at the end of Main Street (which they would do at even greater scale), the park itself would be placed on the far North end of the property to serve as the "carrot" to draw people to travel through EPCOT. Walt would bring Marvin Davis drawings written on paper napkins. A north-south road would connect it all, as Walt had described to Roy the night before he died, while pointing to the tiles on the ceiling. But this carrot concept made the project much more expensive, as simply placing it at the corner of 1-4 and 192 down South would remove the need for creating a large infrastructure of roads and canals.

Roy did not share Walt's enthusiasm for building a future community, but they did agree with the idea that by building the park first, there would then be income flowing to build EPCOT later. Walt also agreed to the location of the Magic Kingdom and even to the idea that the Magic Kingdom would serve as the "carrot" to attract Guests to everything else built later—even at greater expense.

The King of the Magic Kingdom

What made the original concept around EPCOT important is that it would justify a government structure. So, when the film succeeded in persuading legislators to get the needed bills passed in both the Florida House and Senate—with wide majority—Roy came to Florida's capital, Tallahassee, to sign the bills. Governor Claude Kirk (Florida's first Republican governor since Reconstruction) met Roy and led him through the governor's mansion to the garden for signing. Roy's biography states that Kirk "looked quizzically at Roy.

He said, "Roy, I have studied your legislation, I have read it carefully, studied and restudied it. There's one serious omission, and I can't understand it."

Roy was perplexed. "What's that, governor?"

"There's no provision in the kingdom for the crown."

Ray Bradbury once suggested to Walt Disney that he run for mayor of Los Angeles. Walt's retort was, "Why run for mayor when I'm already the king of Disneyland?"

With Walt gone, there would surely be no king at the Magic Kingdom. But that didn't mean it wouldn't bear his name. Many felt that the appropriate title for this East coast operation should be Disney World in the same way it was Disneyland on the West Coast. The word "world" would suggest something much larger than "land."

But Roy wanted it to be *Walt* Disney World, not just Disney World. He had considered how everyone knew Ford cars—even driving them. But no one associated it with Henry Ford, who created it.

In one meeting where Roy was present, someone referred to the project by calling it Disney World. According to his biography, "Roy stopped the individual. His eyes narrowed behind the glasses, and he said firmly. 'I'm only going to say this one more time. I want it called *Walt* Disney World. Not Disney World, not Disneyland, not anything else. *Walt Disney World.*'"

More than a Land: A Real Tomorrowland Prototype

Before you even get to the Magic Kingdom, you have to cross the swamp. Well, that's what it seemed like at the time. Now it's a body of water known as the Seven Seas Lagoon.

But choosing this location for the Magic Kingdom and the associated infrastructure was not a convenient choice. The acreage was largely swamp and could not simply be built upon. It would require dirt. That dirt came from what you see as the body of water in front of the Magic Kingdom, itself simply part of the swamp.

Eight million cubic yards of dirt were taken and piled onto the present site of the Magic Kingdom. Then a labyrinth of buildings and corridors were created on top of the soil to create a utilidor. That was then buried with more dirt, and the Magic Kingdom was built on top.

Standing on Main Street, for example, you are actually standing on the roof of the utilidor. Underneath Main Street, Cast Members, utility vehicles, and supplies are being moved away from the show you are experiencing onstage at the Magic Kingdom. All of Magic Kingdom, with its utilidor included, stands above the water line.

Underneath all of this, and also throughout the resort, are any number of futuristic technologies for its time. These include:

AVAC. An Automated Vacuum-Assisted Collection trash system that sucks trash through pneumatic tubes underneath the park.

Water management systems. Some 43 miles of winding drainage canals with innovative flood-control gates.

Fiber optics. America's first fiber-optic telephone system was employed here.

Wastewater treatment centers. Dedicated water tank facilities allow water hyacinths at Walt Disney World to remove 90 percent of the suspended particles from waste-water effluent.

Energy innovations. Disney's Central Energy Plant was also one of the first in the United States to house boilers and absorption chillers that utilize exhaust heat, to benefit air conditioning, hot water and heating for the parks and resort hotels.

Mass transportation. Linear induction vehicles (PeopleMover) and 14.7 lane miles worth of monorails that handle over 50,000,000 people a year. Along with a massive system of roads and waterways, this truly makes the "World on the Move."

DACS. The Digital Animation Control System provides a centralized location to maintain computer systems all together.

All of this combined to create a very different approach to simply building a theme park. Indeed, it was the foundation for trying out ideas that could lead to the ultimate Tomorrowland.

More than a Park: The Vacation Kingdom of the World

In the wake of all that removed soil was a 200-acre lake known as the Seven Seas Lagoon. This body of water attached itself to the existing Bay Lake, which became the centerpiece for creating a resort destination with major hotels surrounding it. Swimming, boating and other forms of recreation helped to round out the resort experience.

This was hugely important. As Disneyland only required many of its Guests to get on the freeway and drive over from other points of Los Angeles, Walt Disney World needed to promote the idea of not just passing by or staying for a day but staying overnight or a week! Creating this lake allowed Disney to promote Walt Disney World as a resort destination, as opposed to a one-day park experience associated with Disneyland out in California. Adding a monorail around it was not just a means of transportation to connect you to the parking lot (which could have been placed closer to the park) but was a windowed showcase to visiting Guests that they could actually stay here and enjoy a vacation. Indeed, it would be the Vacation Kingdom of the World.

We take for granted the years of construction that created what we experience today. But in the 1960's, this was a monumental undertaking, especially considering that they were building on a swamp. The paradigm back then was that there was little that could ever be done with swamp. With construction and technology, Walt Disney World came out the gate looking like a brand-new Tomorrowland—even before they had created an EPCOT.

Ideas for the Next Century

Consider how you can make the magic come alive for you:

- What opportunities exist where others see little potential?

- Are there paradigms in your business that could be dramatically re-altered?

- How can you maximize your investments to create the greatest possible return?

Opening the Vacation Capital of the World

Getting Everyone on Board

Design and construction went on for some four years following the passing of Walt Disney and the approval of the Reedy Creek Improvement District. But all good projects must cross the finish line and be on time. Getting everyone on board was how it happened.

Labor Day, 1971

When Disneyland opened up in 1955, it was the middle of July. In the days and weeks that followed, over a million people visited the park before the summer ended. It was a successful start to what would be known as "The Happiest Place on Earth." But it was a crash course on managing huge guest numbers.

So, when Magic Kingdom and all of Walt Disney World opened, they decided to do it in the off season, allowing enough time to ramp up to prepare for the holidays and busier times of the year. October 1, 1971, was chosen. But when you choose that date, you are preceded by another holiday—Labor Day. The park was under a tight schedule to open on time. It was all they could do to look ready by October 1st. Park and construction management decided that it was best to work through the holiday weekend. Imagine the conversations with unions:

"We know that it's Labor Day and that it's a holiday weekend, but we need everyone working to get the park opened in time for October 1st!"

The response? "No."

"You don't understand. We are expecting huge crowds to show up on opening day. Press is coming from around the world. This thing will be televised. Everyone will be wondering if we have our act together. We have to work through Labor Day!"

The response? "You don't get it. It's Labor Day. We're not working!"

Management then took a step back and reconsidered their approach. "If we can't get them to *work* on Labor Day, what if we had them *play* on Labor Day?"

To that end, they invited everyone involved in the construction of the Magic Kingdom to bring their family and be management's guests that Labor Day weekend. Management worked the park, using new hires and opening every attraction that was ready for the guests at that point.

Can you imagine the pride on the faces of those construction workers when that little daughter said, "Did you build that castle? It's beautiful! It's amazing!"

Can you also imagine the experience when one of those little kids said, "Hey, look at those submarines from 20,000 Leagues Under the Sea! How cool is…wait a minute, they're not ready to ride yet? How come you haven't finished building that, Dad?!"

At the end of the weekend, management told everyone involved with the construction of the park, "Get us open by October 1st, and when the construction is completed, we will get all of you back in to see the parks again for free."

Do you think the Magic Kingdom opened on time?

Green Side Up

To get things ready for opening, Dick Nunis was ultimately placed in charge of Walt Disney World. To make sure matters were on track, he would meet with the Disney World Operating Committee (DWOC) every morning in one of the construction trailers. The meetings held first thing in the morning became earlier and earlier as deadlines neared. Eventually he moved the meeting to 6 am. The next morning, he found everyone on the committee there on time wearing pajamas. Even Jack Olson, head of merchandising, had a razor and mug in his hand ready to shave, Nunis got the message, and he moved the meetings back to 7 am.

Dick was known by some as "The Temper." He expected others to follow through, and he modeled the same. He didn't intend to be threatening, but if his presence working alongside someone showed the urgency of getting the job done, so be it. The night before the press opening of Walt Disney World, students from Rollins College had been called in to help with tasks for getting the resort ready. With the clock running out, Dick Nunis was out in front of Disney's Contemporary Resort directing these kids to get the sod laid out in patches. Some had never laid sod and asked for greater direction. Dick's reply was, "Green. Side. Up!"

This was the way things were often done during that time. An even better example of this comes not from the Contemporary Resort, but from the streets of Frontierland. In the olden days, frontier towns were kept at peace by a sheriff who oversaw law and order. Often the sheriff was called upon to carry out tough duties others feared accomplishing. In that role, they often carried out jobs beyond policing. Those duties included keeping watch over the jail, removing stray animals, or playing judge.

Naming the Sheriff

In his book, *Spinning Disney's World*, Charles Ridgway talks about how Walt Disney would call on individuals to handle specific assignments that were beyond the call of duty. Walt tapped into individuals to get something done even though it was clearly not part of their expertise. He called it "Naming the Sheriff."

After Walt, the title stayed on. For example, take a look at the red paving found along the streets of Frontierland in the Magic Kingdom of Walt Disney World. Shortly before the opening of Walt Disney World in 1971, Marketing Director Jack Lindquist was named the Sheriff and tasked to fly to Boston. Workers were ready to pour concrete for the red-colored paving throughout the Magic Kingdom, but there was no red coloring powder. It was Friday. And it needed to be available by Monday morning. No problem. Jack spent his weekend on a rescue mission to Boston, chartering a plane, obtaining the colored powder, and arriving just in time for construction work on Monday.

These were the frantic days to get Walt Disney World opened. As shared in *Realityland*, by David Koenig, a delivery truck rolled into the service area behind Tomorrowland. With a major storm coming in, Bob Mathieson gathered people and created a bucket brigade to get the truck unloaded. "It was getting pretty dark, and you didn't even know the guy you're working alongside of. We got this truck unloaded and covered. I went down the line, thanking everyone for coming to help. And at the end of the line is Roy. I said, 'Roy! What are you doing here? 'Well, I came by and saw you needed some help. So, I thought I'd help out a bit.'"

It was that kind of an "all hands-on deck" attitude that made Walt Disney World a reality. Jack Lindquist acted in that way, Dick Nunis planned and managed that way, and Roy Disney especially led by modeling it that way.

Ideas for the Next Century

Consider how you can make the magic come alive for you:

- What does "Green Side Up" look like in your organization?

- What does "Naming the Sheriff" look like in your organization?

- How do you develop a culture of helping to pitch in even when required to do something that isn't necessarily in your job description?

- How do you celebrate those who go the extra mile beyond their regular duties?

- Are you part of the "bucket brigade that makes things happen"?

42

Roy's Last Decisions

Taking a Long View

Walt Disney World opened on time to soft crowds on October 1, 1971. Weeks later a major press event was held. The Friday after Thanksgiving, cars heading to the park were stretched from the entrance gates out south through the entire property to US 192 and beyond to I-4. In time, the Vacation Kingdom of the World became not just a slogan, but truly *the* vacation capital of the world.

Exhaustion and Loss at the End of the Road

Many people sacrificed to make it happen and leading all this sacrifice was the man who gave up retirement to see his brother's dreams come true. Roy was exhausted by the opening of Walt Disney World. He was exasperated at his executives because he felt costs had gone way over. He was trying to bring this entire project to a close without having any debt. That was an important thing to him and to people of that era who had come through the Great Depression. Opening Walt Disney World debt free was critical to Roy Disney.

He was at home when he watched the *Wonderful World of Disney* episode showing the opening of Walt Disney World. What he kept seeing were the empty spaces and places where there were no crowds. It felt like the enthusiasm and the excitement of the park was missing in that television show. And it was because filming happened when the soft opening crowds came at the beginning. Conversely, when Thanksgiving weekend came, there was an enormous attendance bump the Friday after Thanksgiving—recall the crowds were backed up all the way to US 192—and admissions had to be closed early in the day. They had more people on that one day than they had thus far the entire month. So, Roy was on very much a roller coaster of emotion as he was seeing the park finally open and its first days.

Walt and Roy held many things in common but there were also differences in the relationship and moreover there were a lot of tensions. Therefore, many times, especially after the passing of Walt Disney, he really leaned on his brother-in-law, Mitch. But also during this time, Mitch passed away of pancreatic cancer. This was a huge blow to Roy.

Roy and Mitch could sit down and chat for hours not necessarily about business but just about life in general. When Mitch died it took the starch out of Roy, according to his daughter Patty. So, between this Herculean effort of opening Walt Disney World, and now having his best friend pass on, this was an extraordinarily difficult and stressful period for Roy.

In addition, still at this same time, Roy needed to make some important decisions. The annual shareholders meeting was coming up the following February, and Roy was hoping that afterwards he and Edna would take a long cruise to Australia and the Pacific Ocean, hopefully beginning the retirement he had planned to take before Walt passed away.

The Purchase of the Disney Resorts

In the book *Realityland*, David Koenig points out that in order to create a resort experience that would be debt free, Roy had entered into an alliance with US Steel to actually build out the resort rooms and consequently operate the resorts thereafter. US Steel had created a modular approach that would allow them to build the entire room off site down to the towel racks and then slide the hotel room into the infrastructure or frame of the Contemporary and Polynesian resorts, where it would then be ready for operation.

As noted earlier, Walt Disney World was way behind getting ready for opening, but nowhere was this more apparent than at the resorts themselves. This was because of their involvement with the US Steel deal. It wasn't going well. It took an extra couple of months for construction crews to actually complete the resorts. But a loose end that had been nagging at Roy during the experience was the contention between the two parties and getting it open. Roy was concerned about the relationship once it was running a daily operation. US Steel was also frustrated because they had large cost overruns as well as run-ins with the unions. The modular construction was supposed to save money but at the end of the day, each room exceeded what they thought it would cost them.

No side was happy with what was going on. So, in early December Roy arranged a deal with US Steel to take over the hotels from them for $50 million. In addition, Disney saw that they were probably going to spend another 12 million to complete the work yet to be done. All this in the context of the fact that Roy is trying to keep the resort debt free. So, he has to decide between being debt-free and the long-term picture of ownership in the operation of the resorts. The one person he would have discussed this with was Mitch, but he had just passed on.

Roy's decision to purchase the resorts ultimately led to a more unified resort experience, and not one that was divided between two organizations. But the stress came at a price.

A Change of Guard

The second major decision Roy O. Disney made after the opening of Walt Disney World, and just prior to his passing, was who would lead the organization moving forward. This difficult succession decision involved three people: Donn Tatum, Card Walker, and Dick Nunis.

There were several executives that Roy targeted for the overruns that occurred in the construction of the company. In particular, he aimed his frustration at Card Walker. Roy said at one point that he wanted to put into the minutes the overruns that Card Walker had built out. Donn Tatum, however, heard of Roy's request. Donn realized that if those minutes were entered, it would be his responsibility to tell the board that Roy Disney had not heard correctly what had been reported earlier regarding expenses and the decisions that were being made at that time. It would suggest the possibility that Roy Disney was becoming somewhat senile in the process and did not realize that he had approved many of these expenditures that he himself was frustrated with.

The writing of the minutes was not included. Roy had hoped for a dual presidency that might operate the same way he and Walt Disney had operated. But often that doesn't work. Donn would have been happy to accommodate such a partnership since he was a conciliator. But Card's size and demeanor made him much more directive.

Roy O. told his son Roy E. Disney "I've been thinking a lot about who should run the company, and I've decided that it should be Card." He asked his son Roy E. what he thought. Roy liked Donn a whole lot more. Roy acknowledged the same. But he felt that Card should take the lead. Card Walker took over the organization and ran it almost until the last year before Michael Eisner came in.

One final decision Roy made was regarding Dick Nunis, who took the lead in getting Walt Disney World up and running. Dick had a football player "run tackle" style of energy. Dick had made some questionable decisions of his own, but Roy could see Dick was a hard worker who made things happen. That "green side up" mentality made Roy feel that Dick should oversee running both Disneyland and Walt Disney World operations. He would continue that role even after more parks were added in the years to come.

Roy announced these changes. Changes that would have long repercussions. Perhaps he and Edna could finally take that cruise.

195

Another Sad December

It had been six Christmases since Walt had passed. The family tradition was to take the kids and grandchildren to the annual Christmas parade at Disneyland. On that Sunday morning Roy told Edna that he didn't feel great and wouldn't go. Instead, he went back to bed. Edna went with the family to the park. As the family came home later, they found Roy O. Disney sinking into a coma, the result of a massive brain hemorrhage. He died on December 20, 1971, less than three months after he had opened Walt Disney World in the memory of his brother.

Another December passing. Respectively, December would eventually take the lives of Roy and Walt's wives, Edna (1984) and Lillian (1997).

Ideas for the Next Century

Consider how you can make the magic come alive for you:

- What characteristics make a good partner?

- What are the hard decisions you have to make?

- What are the little decisions made along the way that make the big decisions easier?

- What are the consequences of making or not making a decision?

- Who do you have around you to help as a mentor and listener?

- In selecting others, what are the criteria by which you determine their leadership?

- How are you building the next generation of those who will follow after you?

43

50 Happy Years of Entertainment

An Uncertain Milestone

A Golden Celebration

Walt Disney Productions continued. By 1973, Disney had over 21,000 employees and had a gross revenue of $257,751,000 over a nine-month period, nearly 40 million more than the year before. By this time Walt Disney Productions had produced 113 feature-length films since *Snow White and the Seven Dwarfs*. As the *New York Times* headlined it, "Disney Empire is Hardly Mickey Mouse."

Archivist Dave Smith, new to Walt Disney Productions reached out to Card Walker prior to Walt Disney World's opening to certify that the company began on October 16, 1923, and gently reminding him that the company's golden anniversary was only two short years away. But Walt Disney Productions was doing all it could to open Walt Disney World. Those decisions would come afterwards.

And they did come. It was titled *50 Happy Years of Family Entertainment*. It included a 50 Happy Years logo with a Seventies style "happy face" in place of the "0." It played slightly on the yellow smiley icon made popular in the 1960s. The company celebrated with many events.

The fourth edition of the Disney on Parade travel show premiered that year. Created in 1969 to especially promote the building of Walt Disney World, this arena show would include scenes from Mary Poppins, The Country Bears, and of course, Herbie the Love Bug.

The studio worked with Christopher Finch to produce *The Art of Walt Disney*, a stunning and huge coffee table book chronicling the company's first 50 years. The first two printings were sold out in less than three months.

 The New York Public Library for the Performing Arts held a 50th anniversary film retrospective event in the Lincoln Center. The event continued for nearly a month that summer and featured screenings of classic Disney animated and live-action movies and animated shorts.

Robin Hood premiered to a somewhat favorable audience and was Disney's biggest international-grossing film at $18 million. But critics were quick to note how similar it was to other films like *The Jungle Book* and *The Aristocats*. The song "Love" was nominated for Best Song at the Academy Awards. Ironically, it lost to "The Way We Were" from a film of the same name. "The Way We Were" seems to almost suggest how much Disney was still very much the way they were.

On April 8th, "The Walt Disney Story" took over the space of Great Moments with Mr. Lincoln. After guests complained of Abraham Lincoln being removed, they returned the 16[th.] U.S. president in 1975, sharing the theater space with the Disney exhibit which included exact reproductions of Walt's two offices in Burbank. On April 15th of that year, "The Walt Disney Story" opened in the Gulf Hospitality House in Town Square at Magic Kingdom. Its post-show included a model of a major attraction named Western River Expedition. That attraction was similar to Pirates of the Caribbean but with Southwest themes. But it was never built.

Instead, Pirates of the Caribbean opened at the close of 1973 in Caribbean Plaza in the Magic Kingdom of Walt Disney World. This was controversial, because the attraction was not planned for Walt

Disney World. But Guests saw it promoted in their living rooms by the grand showman himself on *Walt Disney's Wonderful World of Color*. Complaints were made at Town Hall, but since it was cheaper than building something like Western River Expedition from scratch, Pirates was copied in part and brought to Florida. Western River would have to wait indefinitely.

Perhaps most importantly, 94 employees who worked with Walt at the Hyperion Studio were honored with a special "Mousecar" at an exclusive event. The back of this once-in-a-lifetime *50 Happy Years* medal read: "My greatest reward is I've been able to build this wonderful organization. And also, to have the public appreciate and accept what we've done all these years. That is a great reward."— Walt Disney.

Card Walker noted: "In 10 years, all of us who came up with Walt will be gone," he said, "and one of my purposes now is really to build the next generation of young people," to carry the torch for "family entertainment of good quality and good taste, in whatever form."

Storm Clouds Ahead

That form would be tested. The year 1973 had its positive moments such as the Paris Peace Accords and the end of the Vietnam War. But other clouds seemed to be gathering. Ironically, just days after Disney released *Robin Hood* in theaters, President Richard M. Nixon, in the swirl of something called Watergate, stood in a news conference on November 17th—in Disney's Contemporary Resort at Walt Disney World, no less—and infamously declared "I'm not a crook!"

Likewise, the first of a series of recessions seemed to play out in that year. This was very much tied to the Oil Crisis, where oil-producing countries sought to create an oil embargo. Almost overnight the price per barrel of oil went up $300. Where people didn't even think about the price of gas, now they were desperate for it, often lining up down the streets of gas stations waiting to fill up. Associated Press showed photos in a number of papers of how Disneyland's parking lot was far emptier than would typically occur. Walt Disney World depended largely on people driving down from the Northeast and the Mid-West, as airline de-regulation didn't occur until a few years later, and Orlando's McCoy airport offered few gates.

Still with high gross company incomes, Donn Tatum and Card Walker exuded: "We are stronger financially, creatively, and organizationally than we have ever been… We shall continue to progress and will emerge from the current period uniquely prepared for further success in the years ahead." Then they shared a quote from Walt: "Recession doesn't deserve the right to exist. There are just too many things to be done…to be bogged down by temporary economic dislocations."

Social, economic, and political challenges defined the arrival of the 50th anniversary for Walt Disney Productions. Later, under the name of The Walt Disney Company, it would define the arrival of its 100th. But between those two points, comes a growth that rivals few other American enterprises. One that would explode across the globe.

End of Volume I

What's Next?

Individuals just like you are trying to figure out their future. J. Jeff Kober has worked with a wide variety of organizations in the private, public, and non-profit sectors to help them grow and develop to the next level. From leadership excellence, to improving employee engagement; from creating highly satisfied customers to developing long-term customer loyalty, we have solutions that will set your Chain Reaction of Excellence in motion.

Need a keynote speaker? Interested in a workshop or seminar? How about a unique online set of tools you and your employees can use every day? Jeff provides not only these offerings but consulting, organizational development, instructional design, and so much more. He gets into the trenches with organizations and helps leaders like you take teams to the next level.

From hospitals to government agencies; from banks to hotels; from associations to universities, Jeff has labored for some forty years to help organizations make real improvements. And he can help you do the same. Just call to discuss your needs and circumstances. He can offer a solution tailored to your unique needs. You can contact Jeff at 407-973-3219, or at jeffkober@gmail.com

Index

Sources & References

Books

Building a Company: Roy O. Disney and the Creation of an Entertainment Empire, by Bob Thomas. New York: Hyperion, 1998.

Disneyland Hotel, The Early Years: 1954-1988, By Donald W. Ballard, Valencia, California: Old Mill Press, 2021.

Disney, Leadership & You, Disney's Hollywood Studios: by J. Jeff Kober. Performance Journeys Publishing, 2017.

Disney's Hollywood Studios: From Show Biz to Your Biz, by J. Jeff Kober. Theme Park Press, 2014.

Disney's World, by Leonard Mosley, New York: Stein and Day, 1985.

Dream It! Do It! My Half-Century Creating Disney's Magic Kingdoms, by Marty Sklar. New York: Disney Editions Deluxe, 2013.

Ink & Paint: The Women of Walt Disney's Animation, by Mindy Johnson. New York: Disney Editions, 2017.

It's Kind of a Cute Story, by Rolly Crump and Jeff Heimbuch. Baltimore, Maryland: Bamboo Forest Publishing, 2012.

Quotable Walt Disney, by Disney Book Group. New York: Disney Editions Deluxe, 2001

One Little Spark! Mickey's Ten Commandments and The Road to Imagineering, by Marty Sklar. New York: Disney Editions, 2015.

Realityland: True-Life Adventures at Walt Disney World, by David Koenig. Irvine, California: Bonaventure Press, 2007.

Remembering Walt: Favorite Memories of Walt Disney, by Amy Boothe Green & Howard E. Green, Hyperion Press, 1999.

South of the Border with Disney: Walt Disney and the Good Neighbor Program, 1941-1948, J. B. Kaufman, New York: Disney Editions, 2022.

Spinning Disney's World: Memories of a Magic Kingdom Press Agent, by Charles Ridgway. New York: The Intrepid Traveler, 2007.

The Art of Walt Disney, by Christopher Finch, Burbank, California: Walt Disney Productions, 1973.

The Disney Films, by Leonard Maltin, New York: Crown Publishing, 1984.

The Disney Revolt: The Great Labor War of Animation's Golden Age, by Jake S. Friedman, Chicago: Chicago Review Press, 2022.

The Disney Studio Story, by Richard Holliss and Brian Sibley, New York: Crown Publishing, 1988.

The Haunted Mansion: From the Magic Kingdom to the Movies, by Jason Surrell. New York: Disney Editions, 2009.

The Illusion of Life—Disney Animation, by Frank Thomas and Ollie Johnston. New York: Disney Editions, 1981.

The Imagineering Story: The Official Biography of Walt Disney Imagineering, Leslie Iwerks, New York: Disney Editions, 2022.

The Making of Walt Disney's Fun and Fancy Free, by J. B. Kaufman, Los Angeles: Hyperion Historical Alliance Press, 2019.

The Walt Disney Studios: A Lot to Remember, by Steven Clark & Rebecca Cline, New York: Disney Editions, 2017.

The Wonderful World of Customer Service at Disney, 2nd Edition, by J. Jeff Kober. Performance Journeys Publishing, 2020.

Tomorrow-Land: The 1964-65 World's Fair and the Transformation of America, by Joseph Tirella, Guilford, Connecticut: Lyons Press, 2014.

Walt's Apprentice: Keeping the Disney Dream Alive, by Dick Nunis, New York: Disney Editions, 2022.

Walt Disney: An American Original, by Bob Thomas. New York: Simon and Schuster, 1976.

Walt Disney: The Triumph of the American Imagination, by Neal Gabler. New York: Alfred A. Knopf, 2006.

Walt Disney's Imagineering Legends and the Genesis of the Disney Theme Park, by Jeff Kurtti. New York: Disney Editions, 2007.

Walt Disney's Snow White and the Seven Dwarfs & the Making of the Classic Film, by Richard Hollis & Brian Sibley, New York: Simon & Schuster, 1987.

Window on Main Street: 35 Years of Creating Happiness at Disneyland Park, by Van Arsdale France. Laughter Publications, Stanbury Press, 1991.

Printed Articles & Theses

An Historical, Descriptive Study of Disney Educational Media as Informative and Entertaining, by James J. Kober, Thesis Presented to the Department of Communications, Brigham Young University, 1991.

"Man who sank the Mark Twain," by Carma Wadley. Deseret News, October 21, 2005.

"Who's the Mystery Man in Epcot's Garage? Neither Woz nor Jobs," by Andy Denhart. Wired, January 31, 2008.

Electronic Media

The Boys: The Sherman Brothers' Story, by Walt Disney Studios Motion Pictures, directed by Jeffrey C. Sherman and Gregory V. Sherman.

Walt Disney and the 1964 World's Fair, Walt Disney Records, 2008.

More Excellence!

WANT MORE FOR YOUR ORGANIZATION? J. JEFF KOBER OFFERS THE FOLLOWING SOLUTIONS FOR TAKING YOUR WORKPLACE TO NEW LEVELS OF EXCELLENCE!

PERFORMANCE JOURNEYS

DISNEY INSIGHTS

WORLD CLASS BENCHMARKING

Real, practical, and proven ideas for improving leadership, employee engagement, the customer experience and more! Our thought leadership offers you insights that will take your organization to the next level!

Best in business ideas from the "Happiest Place on Earth!" Look to Jeff to offer keynotes, seminars, books and more about great ideas from Disney! Better yet, come visit the parks with him and experience the business behind the magic!

Founded by Jeff and former Disney leader Mark David Jones, World Class Benchmarking highlights not only great benchmarking ideas & models from Disney, but also best-of-the-best practices from other great organizations!

PERFORMANCEJOURNEYS.COM   DISNEYINSIGHTS.COM   WORLDCLASSBENCHMARKING.COM

WANT TO BRING GREAT IDEAS BACK TO YOUR WORKPLACE?

Beyond the consulting, books, and workshops, try our new online learning that bring great tools and ideas from many organizations—including Disney—to your workplace! It's our *Excellence and You* series. Visit any of the above websites to learn more! Or just call J. Jeff Kober at 407-973-3219 or JeffKober@gmail.com.

Made in the USA
Las Vegas, NV
14 December 2023

82774680R00118